THE CATASTROPHIC DECLARATION PROPOSAL FOR NATIONAL DISASTERS AND EMERGENCIES

SAFETY AND RISK IN SOCIETY

Additional books in this series can be found on Nova's website under the Series tab.

Additional E-books in this series can be found on Nova's website under the E-book tab.

NATURAL DISASTER RESEARCH, PREDICTION AND MITIGATION

Additional books in this series can be found on Nova's website under the Series tab.

Additional E-books in this series can be found on Nova's website under the E-book tab.

SAFETY AND RISK IN SOCIETY

THE CATASTROPHIC DECLARATION PROPOSAL FOR NATIONAL DISASTERS AND EMERGENCIES

Landon West
and
Adrian Porter
EDITORS

Nova Science Publishers, Inc.

New York

Library of Congress Cataloging-in-Publication Data

ISBN 978-1-61942-264-3

Published by Nova Science Publishers, Inc. † New York

CONTENTS

PREFACE

The Robert T. Stafford Disaster Relief and Emergency Assistance Act (the Stafford Act) authorizes the President to issue major disaster or emergency declarations in response to catastrophes in the United States that overwhelm state and local governments. This book examines concerns expressed by policymakers and experts that current Stafford Act declarations are inadequate to respond to, and recover from, and presents the arguments for and against amending the act to add a catastrophic declaration amendment.

Chapter 1- The Robert T. Stafford Disaster Relief and Emergency Assistance Act (the Stafford Act) is the principal authority governing federal emergency and disaster response in the United States. The act authorizes the President to issue three categories of declaration: (1) major disaster, (2) emergency, or (3) fire assistance declarations in response to incidents that overwhelm the resources of state and local governments. Once a declaration is issued, a wide range of federal disaster assistance becomes available to eligible individuals and households, public entities, and certain nonprofit organizations. Disaster assistance authorized by the Stafford Act is appropriated by Congress and provided through the Disaster Relief Fund.

Chapter 2- The Robert T. Stafford Disaster Relief and Emergency Assistance Act (the Stafford Act) authorizes the President to issue major disaster or emergency declarations in response to catastrophes in the United States that overwhelm state and local governments. Such declarations result in the distribution of a wide range of federal aid to individuals and families, certain nonprofit organizations, and public agencies. Congress appropriates money to the Disaster Relief Fund (DRF), through both annual appropriations and emergency supplemental appropriations, for disaster assistance authorized by the Stafford Act. The Federal Emergency Management Agency (FEMA) within the Department of Homeland Security (DHS) administers most, but not all, of the authority the statute vests in the President.

Chapter 3- The Robert T. Stafford Disaster Relief and Emergency Assistance Act (referred to as the Stafford Act - 42 U.S.C. 5721 et seq.) authorizes the President to issue "major disaster" or "emergency" declarations before or after catastrophes occur. Emergency declarations trigger aid that protects property, public health, and safety and lessens or averts the threat of an incident becoming a catastrophic event. A major disaster declaration, issued after catastrophes occur, constitutes broader authority for federal agencies to provide supplemental assistance to help state and local governments, families and individuals, and certain nonprofit organizations recover from the incident.

Chapter 4- In response to the terrorist attacks of September 11, 2001, Congress and President Bush moved to consolidate numerous federal emergency plans into a single, unified national response plan. The end product of these efforts was the National Response Plan (NRP), which established broad lines of authority for agencies responding to emergencies and major disasters.

Perceived problems with the implementation of the NRP during Hurricane Katrina led Congress to enact the Post-Katrina Management Reform Act (P.L. 109-295) to integrate preparedness and response authorities. The legislation directed DHS to issue a successor plan to the NRP entitled the National Response Framework (NRF). Implemented in March 2008, the NRF establishes a new approach to coordinating federal and nonfederal resources and entities. The Department of Homeland Security (DHS) maintains that the NRF is an improvement over the NRP. Some, however, assert that the NRF is not an improvement because it does not fully address the problems and challenges associated with the NRP.

This report discusses how national response planning documents have evolved over time and describes the authorities that shape the NRF. Several issue areas that might be examined for potential lawmaking and oversight concerning the NRF are also highlighted.

In: The Catastrophic Declaration Proposal... ISBN: 978-1-61942-264-3
Editors: Landon West and Adrian Porter © 2012 Nova Science Publishers, Inc

Chapter 1

CONSIDERATIONS FOR A CATASTROPHIC DECLARATION: ISSUES AND ANALYSIS[*]

Bruce R. Lindsay and Francis X. McCarthy

SUMMARY

The Robert T. Stafford Disaster Relief and Emergency Assistance Act (the Stafford Act) is the principal authority governing federal emergency and disaster response in the United States. The act authorizes the President to issue three categories of declaration: (1) major disaster, (2) emergency, or (3) fire assistance declarations in response to incidents that overwhelm the resources of state and local governments. Once a declaration is issued, a wide range of federal disaster assistance becomes available to eligible individuals and households, public entities, and certain nonprofit organizations. Disaster assistance authorized by the Stafford Act is appropriated by Congress and provided through the Disaster Relief Fund.

Emergency declarations supplement and promote coordination of local and state efforts such as evacuations and protection of public assets. They may also be declared prior to the impact of an incident to protect property, public health and safety and lessen or avert the threat of a major disaster or catastrophe. Major disaster declarations are issued after an incident and constitute broader authority to help states and localities, as

---

[*] This is an edited, reformatted and augmented version of a Congressional Research Service publication, CRS Report for Congress R41884, from www.crs.gov, dated July 6, 2011.

well as families and individuals, recover from the damage caused by the event. Fire assistance declarations provide grants to state and localities to manage fires that threaten to cause major disasters.

Recently there has been discussion that the Stafford Act should be amended to include a fourth category, generally called a "catastrophic declaration." If approved, catastrophic declarations could be invoked for high-profile, large-scale incidents that threaten the lives of many people, create tremendous damage, and pose significant challenges to timely recovery efforts.

This report examines concerns expressed by policymakers and experts that current Stafford Act declarations are inadequate to respond to, and recover from, highly destructive events, and presents the arguments for and against amending the act to add a catastrophic declaration amendment. This report also includes data analyses of past and potential disasters to determine what incidents might be deemed as catastrophic, and explores alternative policy options that might obviate the need for catastrophic declarations.

INTRODUCTION

Numerous studies issued by policy experts, congressional committees, the White House, federal offices of Inspector General, and the Government Accountability Office (GAO), among others, have concluded that the government response to Hurricane Katrina was subject to a variety of deficiencies that occurred at all levels of government.[1] Such deficiencies include questionable leadership decisions and capabilities, organizational failures, overwhelmed preparation and communication systems, and inadequate statutory authorities. Additionally, oversight and investigations into Gulf Coast recovery efforts has led some to conclude that federal recovery assistance has been overly bureaucratic and untimely.[2] Others have argued that the disaster declaration process "does not provide the necessary framework to manage the challenges posed by 21st century catastrophic threats."[3]

These conclusions have led to a number of reforms in federal emergency management laws and policies. For example, one proposed reform currently being contemplated by policymakers is an amendment to the Robert T. Stafford Disaster Relief and Emergency Assistance Act (hereinafter the Stafford Act)[4] that would add a new category of disaster declaration known as a "catastrophic declaration" for events characterized by extraordinary devastation.[5] Proponents of such a measure would argue that adding a catastrophic declaration provision could streamline response and recovery processes and/or possibly increase the amount of federal assistance provided to states and localities after large-scale disasters. Opponents, on the other hand, would argue that implementing a catastrophic declaration is not necessary and may create confusion for emergency managers and officials. States, they say, might be enticed to request a catastrophic declaration rather than a major disaster, if catastrophic declarations trigger an increased federal share of the assistance.

This report examines concerns expressed by policymakers and experts that current Stafford Act declarations are inadequate to respond to, and recover from, highly destructive events, and presents the arguments for and against amending the act to add a catastrophic declaration amendment. These arguments are framed by data analyses of past and potential disasters that might be considered as "catastrophic." The report also explores alternative policy options that might obviate the need for catastrophic declarations.

OVERVIEW OF STAFFORD ACT DECLARATIONS

The Stafford Act is the principal authority governing federal assistance for emergencies and disasters in the United States.[6] The act authorizes the President to issue declarations that trigger federal assistance programs to help states respond to and recover from natural and human-caused incidents.[7] While the Stafford Act authorizes assistance from numerous federal agencies, the Federal Emergency Management Agency (FEMA) is the primary federal agency responsible for coordinating the federal response as well as response activities provided by other agencies and nongovernmental entities.[8]

Two organizing principles guide the declaration process. First is the preservation of the governor's discretion to request federal assistance. Second is the President's discretion to decide to issue or deny the request for federal assistance.

The President cannot issue either an emergency or a major disaster declaration without a gubernatorial request. The only exception to this rule is the authority given to the President to declare an emergency when the President "determines that an emergency exists for which the primary responsibility for response rests with the United States because the emergency involves a subject area for which, under the Constitution or laws of the United States, the United States can exercise exclusive or preeminent responsibility and authority."[9] The Stafford Act stipulates several procedural actions a governor must take prior to requesting federal disaster assistance.

The governor cannot request a declaration unless he or she determines the event has overwhelmed the state's resources to such an extent that federal resources are needed.

The Stafford Act authorizes three types of presidential declarations—the proposal for a catastrophic declaration would add a fourth type of declaration. The three currently authorized by the Stafford Act include (1) Fire Management Assistance Grant Program declarations (FMAGP), (2) emergency declarations, and (3) major disaster declarations.

Fire Management Assistance Grant Program Declarations

While the President has the sole authority to issue an emergency or major disaster declaration, the determination to issue a FMAGP declaration can be rendered either by the President or FEMA.[10] A FMAGP declaration authorizes various forms of federal assistance, such as equipment, personnel, and grants to any state or local government for the control, management and mitigation of any fire on public or private forest land or grassland that might become a major disaster.[11]

Emergency Declarations

The Stafford Act defines an emergency broadly as

> any occasion or instance for which, in the determination of the President, federal assistance is needed to supplement State and local efforts and capabilities to save lives and to protect property and public health and safety, or to lessen or avert the threat of a catastrophe in any part of the United States.[12]

Emergency declarations authorize activities that can help states and communities carry out essential services as well as activities that might reduce the threat of future damage. Emergency declarations, however, do not provide assistance for repairs and replacement of public infrastructure or nonprofit facilities.[13] Emergency declarations may be declared before an incident occurs to save lives and prevent loss. For example, emergency declarations have been declared prior to a hurricane making landfall to help state and local governments take steps (evacuation assistance, placement of response resources, etc.) that might lessen the impact of the storm and prevent a major disaster from occurring.[14]

Major Disaster Declarations

While emergencies are defined broadly, the Stafford Act defines a major disaster narrowly as:

> any natural catastrophe (including any hurricane, tornado, storm, high water, wind-driven water, tidal wave, tsunami, earthquake, volcanic eruption, landslide, mudslide, snowstorm, or drought), or, regardless of cause, any fire, flood, or explosion, in any part of the United States, which in the determination of the President causes damage of sufficient severity and magnitude to warrant major disaster assistance under this chapter to supplement the efforts and available resources of states, local governments, and disaster relief organizations in alleviating the damage, loss, hardship, or suffering caused thereby.[15]

The definition for a major disaster is more precise than an emergency declaration, and the range of assistance available to state and local governments, private, nonprofit organizations, and families and individuals is much broader. Under a major disaster declaration, state and local governments and certain nonprofit organizations are eligible (if so designated) for assistance for the repair or restoration of public infrastructure such as roads and buildings. A major disaster declaration may also include additional programs beyond temporary housing such as disaster unemployment assistance and crisis counseling. A major disaster declaration may also include recovery programs such as community disaster loans.

PROPOSED CATASTROPHIC DECLARATION

If amended, the Stafford Act might provide a declaration for what might be classified as a "mega-disaster" or "catastrophic disaster." It is unclear, however, what differentiates a disaster from a catastrophe. Moss and Shelhamer, two policy scholars who have written on the subject, state that catastrophic incidents by definition, tend to occur in large metropolitan regions due to the concentration of people and infrastructure. For example, a category 5 hurricane striking an undeveloped coast will generate less damage than a category 3 hurricane hitting a major city. Recent catastrophes include the 1989 Loma Prieta Earthquake (San Francisco), the 1994 Northridge Earthquake (Los Angeles), Hurricane Hugo (1989), Hurricane Andrew (1992), Hurricanes Katrina and Rita (2005), the Midwest Floods of 1993, and the September 11 attacks of 2001.[16]

The authors then recommend amending Section 102 of the Stafford Act with the language used to define a catastrophic incident in the Post-Katrina Emergency Management Reform Act of 2006 (Title VI of the Department of Homeland Security Appropriations Act, 2007—hereinafter the Post-Katrina Act).[17] The Post-Katrina Act defines a catastrophic incident broadly as

> any natural disaster, act of terrorism, or other man-made disaster that results in extraordinary levels of casualties or damage or disruption severely affecting the population (including mass evacuations), infrastructure, environment, economy, national morale, or government functions in an area.[18]

The above definition was used in the Post-Katrina Act for the purposes of improving planning documents by defining the scope of events that should be considered by the Catastrophic Incident Annex of the National Response Framework (NRF).[19] The definition was not used in the context of actual declared disasters nor was it intended to replace the definition of a major disaster in the Stafford Act.

The main difference between a catastrophic incident as defined in the Post-Katrina Act and the definition of a major disaster in the Stafford Act is that the former focuses on the event's scope, impact, and severity. In general, a catastrophic incident would carry far-reaching consequences beyond a state's borders and have national implications including the economy, infrastructure, and even national psyche. In contrast, the major disaster definition generally focuses more on categorizing causes that potentially overwhelm states and localities.

Supporters of catastrophic declarations argue that while "routine disasters" can be managed through major disaster declarations, large-scale, destructive incidents warrant their own type of declaration because they pose unique challenges inadequately addressed by major disaster declarations. Examples of such challenges may include

- The President can declare an emergency without a gubernatorial request, if he considers the event to be primarily a federal responsibility, but must wait for a gubernatorial request for most emergencies and all major disasters.[20] The wait for a request could delay the federal response, or federal assistance, or both.
- The response and recovery efforts associated with large-scale disasters involve multiple federal agencies that require higher levels of leadership to resolve potential inter-agency conflicts, and effectively coordinate and manage response and recovery efforts.
- Current response and recovery procedures for major disasters are too cumbersome for large-scale disasters because the procedures are too rigid and inefficient to provide assistance at an accelerated rate.
- Some argue that federal assistance is needed more quickly after large-scale, destructive incidents than routine disasters—the disbursal of assistance provided through a major disaster declaration is too slow to meet recovery needs.
- Due to the enormous amount of destruction and the economic impacts caused by large-scale disasters, many states and localities are unable to pay their portion of the cost-share.

The following section describes how a catastrophic declaration might address these challenges.

POTENTIAL USES AND BENEFITS OF A CATASTROPHIC DECLARATION

A catastrophic declaration may be used to trigger certain mechanisms before, during, and after a catastrophe. Policymakers might also elect to apply a catastrophic declaration to one or more phases of the incident.

Prior to an Incident

The Catastrophic Incident Annex of the NRF states federal resources and assets may be deployed prior to a catastrophic incident in anticipation of a request from state, tribal, and local governments that an imminent disaster appears to threaten human health and safety.[21] Such activities may include the placing of resources to reduce the impact of the incident and improve response capabilities, pre-positioning of emergency and disaster employees and supplies, monitoring the status of the situation, communicating with state emergency officials on potential assistance requirements, and deploying teams and resources to maximize the speed and effectiveness of the anticipated federal response.

As mentioned previously, under certain conditions the Stafford Act authorizes federal support in the absence of a gubernatorial request to "save lives, prevent human suffering, or mitigate severe damage." If Congress chose to create a catastrophic declaration, it might elect to amend Section 402 to provide the President with similar authority so as to trigger federal activities such the ones described above. Additionally, the amendment could be designed to signal the immediate deployment of federal strike teams and surge capacity forces.[22] Alternatively, some may argue the Stafford Act could be amended to authorize the aforementioned precautionary measures for major disasters without a catastrophic declaration.

During an Incident

The NRF provides the guiding principles for a unified response by assigning roles and responsibilities to all levels of government, nongovernmental organizations, the private sector, communities, and communities to all types of hazards regardless of their origin. The unified response is executed through supporting documents known as annexes: Emergency Support Functions (ESF) Annexes and Incident Annexes.[23]

ESFs group federal agencies by their resource and function related to a particular incident. For example, all federal agencies that play a role in the response and recovery of an oil spill are listed in ESF #10. The ESF's function is to designate lead and supporting federal agencies responsible for incident response and recovery.

Similar to an ESF, Incident Annexes group agencies by matching their resources and functions to a particular incident. Incident Annexes also designate lead and support agencies. For example, federal agencies responsible for response and recovery from a biological attack are listed in the Biological Incident Annex. Incident Annexes differ from an ESF, however, because the incidents they address have been deemed to require specialized response and recovery activities specific to the incident.

Response and recovery efforts carried out under each ESF and Incident Annex are executed through various operational plans. Proponents would argue that a catastrophic declaration could be used to trigger streamlined procedures within these operational plans. They may further argue that catastrophic incidents create tremendous uncertainty and that bureaucratic protocols exacerbate this uncertainty and hinder efforts aimed at a timely response. Thus, streamlining procedures might provide flexibility to operational plans and promote autonomous decision-making.

On the other hand, some may argue that, while intuitively appealing, providing additional flexibility during a catastrophic declaration might produce a chaotic federal response because operational plans among federal agencies are tightly coupled with each other. Deviation in response by one agency could have negative rippling effects that could hinder the response of other agencies.

After an Incident

A catastrophic declaration could be used to automatically alter aspects of recovery polices and regulations. Such a declaration could have triggers that would cause a change in the percentage of federal resources as well as adjusting the delivery system of traditional disaster relief programs. The following recovery strategies might be included in the event of a catastrophic declaration.

- The catastrophic declaration could automatically increase the federal cost-share to lessen the economic impact states and localities incur from catastrophic incidents. The Stafford Act provides that the federal share for the repair, restoration, and replacement of damaged facilities "shall be not less than 75%."[24] A catastrophic declaration could be used to automatically increase the federal share to 90% or perhaps 100%. Moreover, the 72-hour window of 100% funding for immediate federal aid could be extended for a longer period. Early knowledge of such adjustments may accelerate state and local activity because foreknowledge of the adjustment provides states and localities with an assurance of fiscal relief which would then encourage them to act quickly to accomplish necessary repairs and begin comprehensive recovery planning. However, these adjustments can add significantly to the overall cost of the disaster.[25]

- A catastrophic declaration could trigger a number of changes to recovery programs that could speed assistance and provide increased flexibility. Some of these changes could include the delivery of block grants to states to handle immediate needs and begin infrastructure repairs. An alternative would be for a catastrophic event to (1) switch on "gap funding" which provides timely front-end funding to states and localities to cover initial efforts; (2) make straight-time force[26] account labor (for disaster work) by state and local governments eligible for reimbursement; (3) automatically increase funding caps for the Community Disaster Loan (CDL) program;[27] and (4) provide clear authority and resources to FEMA and its federal partners for long-term recovery efforts in partnership with state and local governments.
- Once declared, catastrophic declarations could trigger certain congressional rules that might prevent potential deadlock over the passage of disaster relief funds for disaster-stricken communities.

On the other hand, it could be argued that the Stafford Act could be amended to make these changes part of a major disaster declaration.

ANALYSIS OF CONGRESSIONAL ACTION AFTER THE INCIDENT

Part of the argument for a catastrophic declaration is that it could provide immediate financial assistance on a broader scale without having to await congressional approval for additional federal assistance through a supplemental appropriation. An examination of the record, however, demonstrates that congressional action on emergency supplemental funding in the wake of large disasters has grown more rapid in recent years (see *Table 1*).

It could be argued that Congress has acted expeditiously. On average, Congress has passed supplemental appropriations for disaster assistance within 33 days of the disaster declaration. It can also be argued that while resources may be provided relatively quickly for routine disasters, catastrophic incidents require an accelerated timeframe to provide adequate assistance. In addition, the results of this analysis indicate that Congress has been responsive to the largest and most devastating incidents. In some cases, disaster assistance was enacted within one week of the declaration.

Table 1. Emergency Supplemental Funding for Large Disasters

Event	Date of Declaration	Congressional Action	Days
Hurricane Katrina	August 29, 2005	September 2, 2005	3
Hurricane Isabel	September 18, 2003	September 30, 2003	12
9/11 Terrorist Attacks	September 11, 2001	September 18, 2001	7
Nisqually Earthquake	March 1, 2001	July 24, 2001	114
Hurricane Floyd	September 16, 1999	October 20, 1999	34
Northridge Earthquake	January 17, 1994	February 12, 1994	26
Midwest Floods	June 11, 1993	August 12, 1993	62
Hurricane Andrew	August 23, 1992	September 23, 1992	31
Hurricane Hugo	September 20, 1989	September, 29, 1989	9

Source: CRS Report R40708, Disaster Relief Funding and Emergency Supplemental
Appropriations, by Bruce R. Lindsay and Justin Murray.
Note: Table 1 reflects the number of days it took to enact the first supplemental
appropriation. Some incidents (such as Hurricane Katrina) received more than one
supplemental appropriation for disaster relief.

Moreover, while it took longer than 30 days to enact some supplemental
appropriations, the incidents for which the funding was enacted generally had
fewer damages than the larger, more expensive disasters.

The reaction to the devastation caused by the 2005 hurricane season
resulted in historic amounts of disaster response and recovery funding. Along
with the amount of resources provided by Congress, it could be argued that the
Stafford Act is a very flexible instrument that provides broad authority for
various forms of assistance. The reluctance or inability of some to administer
these authorities in the past does not eliminate their existence or the possible
help that can be derived from those broad authorities under any disaster
declaration. Authorities such as Section 402 of Stafford for "General Federal
Assistance" and Section 403 for "Essential Assistance" provide FEMA the
discretion to use various forms of federal help or to supplement state help to
achieve disaster response and recovery goals.[28]

ANALYSIS OF CATASTROPHIC EVENTS PAST AND FUTURE

This section analyzes incidents that might be deemed as catastrophic to
help frame a debate concerning the need and desirability of amending the
Stafford Act to include a catastrophic declaration. Because catastrophic
incidents are generally characterized as events that cause extraordinary

damage, or loss of life (or both), the following analysis is based on data from past, large-scale incidents that have occurred in the United States, as well as data derived from studies that predict damage levels and loss of life for large-scale disasters that could happen in the future (see *Table 2*). [29]

This report incorporates a method known as the value of statistical life (VSL) to assign a monetary value to each fatality caused by the given incident.[30] VSL helps compare incidents with many fatalities and little damage (such as the Chicago Heat Wave of 1995) to incidents that caused significant damages, but had few, or no, fatalities (such as the Love Canal incident in 1978).

This section of the report is divided into four subsections that rank incidents according to the following: (1) previous large-scale disasters by estimated damage costs; (2) previous large-scale disasters by estimated damage and VSL costs; (3) previous large-scale disasters and potential incidents by damage costs; and (4) previous large-scale disasters and potential incidents by estimated damage and VSL costs.

The percentiles used for this analysis are derived by multiplying the costliest incident in the subsection by a given percentile.[31] It should be noted that the data used for this analysis are subject to variations and limitations (see "Caveats and Methodology").

Previous Incidents with Extraordinary Damages

This subsection ranks some of the costliest incidents to ever occur in the United States in the past 140 years (*Table 3*). Assuming catastrophic incidents are the most expensive events, then the following conclusions could be drawn: If the 90th percentile ($151 billion or more in damages) of incidents are catastrophic, then only the 1871 Chicago Fire would qualify as a catastrophic incident. If the 80th percentile ($134 billion or more in damages) of incidents are catastrophic, only the 1871 Chicago Fire and Hurricane Katrina would qualify as catastrophic incidents. These would remain constant until the 20th percentile ($34 billion or more in damages), which would then include the September 11, 2001 terrorist attacks. The remaining incidents fall below the 20th percentile.

Table 2. Previous and Potential Catastrophic Incidents, Through 2008
(2010 dollars)

Disaster	Fatalities	Value of Statistical Life (VSL)	Damage Estimate	Combined VSL and Damage Estimate
1871 Chicago Fire	300	1,800,000,000	168,000,000,000	169,800,000,000
1900 Galveston Hurricane	9,000	54,000,000,000	700,000,000	54,700,000,000
1906 San Francisco Earthquake	3,000	18,000,000,000	9,579,792,048	27,579,792,048
1919 Influenza Pandemic	675,000	4,050,000,000,000	0	4,050,000,000,000
1929 Great Mississippi Flood	1,000	6,000,000,000	2,899,905,508	8,899,905,508
1964 Alaska Earthquake/Tsunami	131	786,000,000	311,000,000	1,097,000,000
1969 Hurricane Camille	256	486,000,000	1,421,000,000	1,886,000,000
1965 Hurricane Betsy	81	1,536,000,000	1,400,000,000	2,957,000,000
1974 Xenia (Easter) Tornado Outbreak	330	1,980,000,000	1,000,000,000	2,980,000,000
1978 Love Canal	0	0	400,000,000	400,000,000
1980 Mount St. Helens	57	342,000,000	1,000,000,000	1,342,000,000
1989 Loma Prieta Earthquake	63	342,000,000	10,000,000,000	7,342,000,000
1992 Hurricane Andrew	23	378,000,000	27,000,000,000	10,378,000,000
1995 Chicago Heat Wave	525	138,000,000	0	27,138,000,000
1989 Hurricane Hugo	57	360,000,000	7,000,000,000	20,360,000,000
1994 Northridge Earthquake	60	3,150,000,000	20,000,000,000	3,150,000,525
2001 September 11th Terrorist Attacks	2,978	17,868,000,000	42,600,000,000	60,468,000,000
2005 Hurricane Katrina	1,833	10,998,000,000	148,000,000,000	158,998,000,000
2008 Hurricane Ike	20	120,000,000	19,300,000,000	19,420,000,000
ARkStorm[a]	1,000	6,000,000,000	400,000,000,000	406,000,000,000

Table 2. (Continued)

Disaster	Fatalities	Value of Statistical Life (VSL)	Damage Estimate	Combined VSL and Damage Estimate
New Madrid Earthquake[b]	85,000	510,000,000,000	120,000,000,000	630,000,000,000
Southern San Andreas Fault Earthquake[b]	1,800	10,800,000,000	200,000,000,000	210,800,000,000

Source: Data derived from supplemental appropriations and government studies and reports. See the Appendix for a full list of the sources used for this table.

[a] ARkStorm is a hypothetical flood disaster that could occur (see footnote 35).

[b] Denotes a hypothetical earthquake that could occur (see Appendix).

Table 3. Prior Large-Scale Disasters by Damage Estimate, through 2008 (2010 dollars)

Disaster	Damage Estimate	Rank
1871 Chicago Fire	168,000,000,000	1
1 90th Percentile (≥ $151 billion) 1		
2005 Hurricane Katrina	148,000,000,000	2
1 80th Percentile (≥ $134 billion) 1		
2001 September 11th Terrorist Attacks	42,600,000,000	3
1 20th Percentile (≥ $34 billion) 1		
1992 Hurricane Andrew	27,000,000,000	4
1994 Northridge Earthquake	20,000,000,000	5
2008 Hurricane Ike	19,300,000,000	6
1989 Loma Prieta Earthquake	10,000,000,000	7
1906 San Francisco Earthquake	9,579,792,048	8
1989 Hurricane Hugo	7,000,000,000	9
1929 Great Mississippi Flood	2,899,905,508	10
1969 Hurricane Camille	1,421,000,000	11
1965 Hurricane Betsy	1,400,000,000	12
1974 Xenia (Easter) Tornado Outbreak	1,000,000,000	13
1980 Mount St. Helens	1,000,000,000	14
1900 Galveston Hurricane	700,000,000	15
1978 Love Canal	400,000,000	16
1964 Alaska Earthquake/Tsunami	311,000,000	17

Source: Data derived from supplemental appropriations and government studies and reports. See Appendix. sources for a full list of the sources used for this table.

Methodology: $168,000,000,000 x 0.90 = $151,200,000,000, $168,000,000,000 x 0.80 = $134,400,000,000, and $168,000,000,000 x 0.20 = $33,600,000,000. Some figures have been rounded. The 1995 Chicago Heat Wave is not included in Table 3.

Figure 1 presents the same data in chronological order. Again, assuming catastrophic incidents are the most expensive events, then the following conclusions could be drawn: over 130 years has elapsed between the most expensive incident (the 1871 Chicago Fire) and the second and third most expensive incidents (Hurricane Katrina, and the September 11, 2001 terrorist attacks, respectively). However, many of the most expensive disasters have occurred in more recent times. In the last 30 years, at least six incidents that had damages of $10 billion or more have occurred, and in the last 16 years, at least five incidents that had damages of $19 billion or more have occurred.

(2010 dollars)

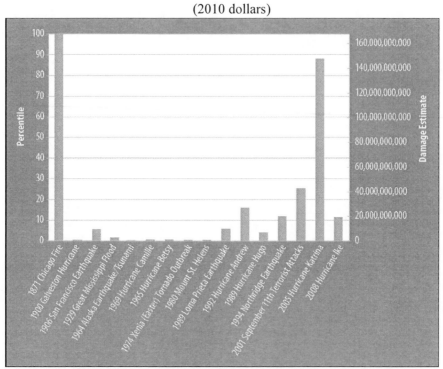

Source: Data derived from supplemental appropriations and government studies and reports. See the Appendix for a full list of the sources used for this figure.
Methodology: See methodological description in Table 3.

Figure 1. Previous Large-Scale Disasters by Damage Estimate, through 2008.

Given the number of large-scale disasters occurring in the last 30 years, one might conclude that large-scale disasters are occurring more frequently—which might support an argument for a catastrophic declaration. A counterargument, on the other hand, is that in terms of damage costs, only Hurricane Katrina truly qualifies as a catastrophic event when compared to other, recent incidents. It might be further argued that while many of the most expensive disasters have occurred in recent years, the increased costs associated with such incidents are a function of variables that are not necessarily related to the magnitude of the incidents (such as increased federal expenditures for assistance and recovery projects, the replacement of expensive infrastructure, and the development of previously uninhabited areas). Consequently, opponents of a catastrophic declaration might conclude that damage costs are not a suitable determinant for assessing the need for the new declaration because it fails to address the response and recovery issues previously discussed in this report.

Previous Incidents by VSL and Damage Costs

Table 4 lists the same incidents presented in Table 2 ranked according to combined VSL and damage costs. Assuming that catastrophic incidents are incidents with the highest combined VSL and damage costs, then the following conclusions could be drawn: If the 90th percentile ($153 billion or more) of incidents are catastrophic, then the 1871 Chicago Fire and Hurricane Katrina would qualify as catastrophic incidents. These events would remain singular until the 30th percentile ($51 billion or more) in which the September 11th terrorist attacks and the 1900 Galveston Hurricane would then also qualify as catastrophic. The 1906 San Francisco Earthquake and Fire, the 1995 Chicago Heat Wave, the 1989 Hurricane Hugo, and 2008 Hurricane Ike would all be deemed catastrophic if the 20th percentile were used ($17 billion or more) for the determination.

Figure 2 presents the data from *Table 4* in chronological order. Using the above VSL and damage cost assumptions from above to examine large-scale incidents over the past 140 years, the analysis suggests that approximately 100 years has elapsed between the highest ranked disaster (the 1871 Chicago Fire) and the second highest ranked disaster (Hurricane Katrina).

Additionally, whereas this analysis on damage costs alone might indicate that the "worst" disasters have occurred within the last 30 years, some might conclude that combining VSL with damage costs tends to support the opposite conclusion—that the worst disasters occurred around the turn of the century. Based on the latter conclusion, some may question the need for catastrophic declarations for contemporary incidents. On the other hand, others may argue that recent incidents should still be taken into consideration when evaluating the need for catastrophic declarations. This is because two of the four highest ranked disasters have occurred within the last ten years.

Table 4. Previous Large-Scale Disasters by Combined VSL and Damage Estimates (2010 dollars)

Disaster	Combined VSL and Damage Estimate	Rank
1871 Chicago Fire	169,800,000,000	1
2005 Hurricane Katrina	158,998,000,000	2
1 90th Percentile (≥ $153 Billion) 1		
2001 September 11th Terrorist Attacks	60,468,000,000	3
1900 Galveston Hurricane	54,700,000,000	4
1 30th Percentile (≥ $51 Billion) 1		
1906 San Francisco Earthquake	27,579,792,048	5
1995 Chicago Heat Wave	27,138,000,000	6
1989 Hurricane Hugo	20,360,000,000	7
2008 Hurricane Ike	19,420,000,000	8
1 20th Percentile (≥ $17 Billion) 1		
1992 Hurricane Andrew	10,378,000,000	9
1929 Great Mississippi Flood	8,899,905,508	10
1989 Loma Prieta Earthquake	7,342,000,000	11
1994 Northridge Earthquake	3,150,000,525	12
1974 Xenia (Easter) Tornado Outbreak	2,980,000,000	13
1965 Hurricane Betsy	2,957,000,000	14
1969 Hurricane Camille	1,886,000,000	15
1980 Mount St. Helens	1,342,000,000	16
1964 Alaska Earthquake/Tsunami	1,097,000,000	17
1978 Love Canal	400,000,000	18

Source: Data derived from supplemental appropriations and government studies and reports. See the Appendix for a full list of the sources used for this table.

Methodology: $169,800,000,000 x 0.90 = $152,820,000,000, $169,800,000,000 x 0.30 = $50,940,000,000, and $169,800,000,000 x 0.10 = $16,980,000,000. Some figures have been rounded.

Disasters Past and Future

When the analysis is extended to capture all of the incidents in *Table 2*,[32] the inclusion of potential disasters changes the order of percentile rankings. However, the number of incidents meeting certain catastrophic thresholds remains low.

In terms of damage costs alone, if one assumes catastrophic incidents are the most expensive events, then the following conclusions could be drawn: If the 90th percentile ($360 billion or more) of incidents are catastrophic, then only the hypothetical "ARkStorm" would qualify as a catastrophic incident.

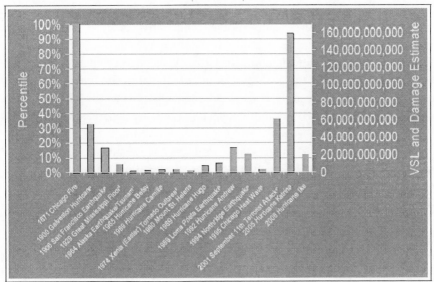

Source: Data derived from supplemental appropriations and government studies and
    reports. See the Appendix for a full list of the sources used for this figure.
Methodology: See the methodological description in Table 4.

Figure 2. Previous Large-Scale Disasters by Combined VSL and Damage Estimates,
Through 2008.

This event would remain singular until the 50th percentile ($200 billion or
more) in which the hypothetical Southern San Andreas Fault Earthquake
would also qualify as catastrophic. If the catastrophic incident threshold
includes incidents in the 40th percentile ($160 billion or more) or higher, then
the 1871 Chicago Fire would be included as catastrophic. [33]

When the highest combined VSL and damage costs are included, the
following conclusions could be drawn: If the 90th percentile ($567 billion or
more) of incidents are catastrophic, then only the New Madrid Earthquake
scenario would qualify as a catastrophic incident. This event would remain
singular until the 60th percentile ($378 billion or more), in which the
ARkStorm would be considered catastrophic. The 30th percentile would
include the Southern San Andreas Fault Earthquake Scenario. All of the
remaining incidents fall under the 10th percentile range ($63 billion or more). [34]

Summary of Analysis and Policy Implications

Upon reviewing the results of the comparative analysis of destructive incidents, it could be argued that highly destructive events occur too rarely to warrant a catastrophic declaration. In terms of damage estimates alone, only one incident exceeds the 90th percentile benchmark, and only two would qualify if the 80th percentile is used as a benchmark (the 1871 Chicago Fire and Hurricane Katrina). In addition, these events are separated by over 130 years.

Similar conclusions might be drawn on the comparative analysis of combined VSL and damage estimate costs—specifically, that high-impact events are too infrequent to merit the addition of a new declaration category— only two incidents in the last 100 years meets the 90th percentile threshold— and these incidents are over 100 years apart from each other. Additionally, the threshold would have to be adjusted to the 30th percentile to include more than two incidents. Critics of the additional declaration might further argue that VSL is a poor determinant for a catastrophic declaration because federal assistance is predominately tied to recovery projects rather than victim or survivor compensation.

With regard to recent disaster activity, proponents who support the addition of a catastrophic declaration could argue that, in terms of damage estimates, 8 of the top 18 incidents have occurred within the last 30 years. However, in terms of combined VSL and damage estimate costs, two of the top four incidents have occurred within the last 10 years. To some, this may be taken as an indication that catastrophic incidents are increasing in frequency. They may also argue that future disasters might be more destructive due to increases in population, development, and infrastructure. Thus, they might argue the scope of this analysis should be limited to more recent incidents. Proponents who support the addition of a catastrophic declaration could also argue that the analysis fails to take into account potential future incidents.

While opponents of a catastrophic declaration might conclude that this analysis demonstrates that catastrophic incidents are too rare to warrant a new type of declaration, supporters might make the claim that the damage and VSL costs portrayed in this analysis would have been reduced if carried out according to the provisions provided under a catastrophic declaration.

Caveats and Methodology

The data sources for the above analyses have been assembled from multiple governmental sources and are listed in the *Appendix*. As mentioned previously, the data on fatalities and damages from these sources are subject to variation and should not be viewed as definitive. Additionally, many studies report death tolls in ranges for various incidents. For the purposes of this report, the average number between the range was used as a fatality figure. The hypothetical scenarios used for the analyses do not represent the universe of possible incidents—such as a nuclear detonation, an asteroid incident, or another influenza pandemic.

There were also some reporting anomalies. The United States Geological Survey (USGS) ARkStorm scenario study did not provide a fatality estimate.[35] For the purposes of this report, the number of fatalities from the 1929 Mississippi flood was used because reporting no deaths produced outlying figures that skewed the data results. Similarly, the 1919 Influenza Pandemic was eliminated from the analyses because the number of fatalities (675,000) produced an outlying figure that skewed the data results.

The comparative analysis spans over a century and the incident computations reported in the analyses do not reflect increases in development, infrastructure, and populations that would have made earlier incidents more costly were they to occur in this period of time. The computations in this report do not reflect current mitigation and response mechanisms that might have decreased the impacts of previous events had they been available.

VSL computations vary among federal agencies from roughly $5 million to $10 million per individual. While FEMA does not use a VSL computation, the Department of Homeland Security (DHS) uses a VSL of $6 million per individual for certain attack scenarios. The VSL value used by DHS was used for this report.

As mentioned previously, damage costs are not the sole determinant for disaster declarations. The purpose of these analyses is to develop a model to determine which incidents could be deemed as catastrophic based on damages and VSL costs. Other considerations, such as potential economic or social impacts of the incidents are not reflected in the analyses. Statistically reliable forecasts of the occurrence of future events based on this data could not be completed due to insufficient data points.

The data presented in this report are not definitive and should be interpreted with care before drawing any conclusions.

SUMMARY OF POTENTIAL IMPLICATIONS

Potential Benefits of a Catastrophic Declaration

Depending on its design, certain benefits may be derived from using a catastrophic declaration for large-scale disasters, including

- accelerated and more robust federal assistance to states prior to an incident,
- the use of specialized response plans and guidelines for the federal response,
- the elimination or reduction of procedures and protocols that might impede response and recovery activities and efforts,
- the elimination or reduction of procedures and protocols that might delay the disbursal of federal assistance, and
- increasing the amount of federal assistance through various mechanisms to help states recovery more quickly and avoid economic hardship.

Potential Drawbacks of a Catastrophic Declaration

The potential drawbacks of a catastrophic declaration may include

- unclear authority and responsibility designations could confuse those responsible for executing the response and recovery,
- increased federal costs for disaster assistance due to increased declaration activity,
- increased federal costs for disaster assistance due to the increased federal cost-share provisions included with the declaration, and
- increased federal involvement and responsibility for incident response.

FURTHER CONSIDERATIONS

Some may argue that the Stafford Act's broad definition of an emergency lacks sufficient specific criteria and provides the President with too much discretion to determine which incidents are emergencies. This, in turn, may have increased the federal role (and by extension—the amount of federal expenditures for disaster assistance) in emergency assistance through declaration "creep." Critics assert that once an incident qualifies as an emergency, the odds are improved that a similar incident in the future will be declared as an emergency. The Post-Katrina Act also uses a broad definition to define a catastrophe. It could be argued that the addition of a broad definition of a catastrophe could also lead to declaration "creep" of major disasters.

The use of an arithmetical formula or sliding scale based on income or population to declare a major disaster or an emergency is precluded by Section 320 of the Stafford Act. Amending the Stafford Act to include a catastrophic declaration would be presumably be subject to the same limitation—unless the amendment requires some form of measurable criteria to be applied.

One method that could be used to keep assistance costs down is legislative language that allows a catastrophic declaration to be downgraded to a major disaster if it was determined that damages did not merit a catastrophic declaration. Downgrading a catastrophic declaration, however, may appear indecisive and create confusion.

Another consideration involves aspects of politics more than policy. It may be difficult for the President to deny a request for a catastrophic declaration because the President might be seen as failing to properly respond to a calamitous event—even if it were declared a disaster.

The predecessor to the NRF, the National Response Plan (NRP) contained guidelines for an "Incident of National Significance" which was intended as a triggering mechanism for various levels of response activities. It was eliminated however, because the designation caused confusion during the Hurricane Katrina response—primarily because the designation established a different leadership structure than was commonly used for "routine" disasters.[36] One the one hand, a catastrophic declaration could be designed to trigger a chain of command structure consisting of higher levels of leadership and rank to address the catastrophe. On the other hand, altering the command structure could create conflicts and confusion because it may be unclear as to who is in charge of the incident. Similarly, a catastrophic declaration designed to alter the response in some manner could also create additional layers of bureaucracy that impede or hinder the response.

Some may argue a catastrophic incident would not receive unique resources that are not already authorized and provided for a major disaster declaration. If this is the case, one might question the need for catastrophic declarations.

A full federal cost-share, if included in a catastrophic declaration, might tempt states to request a catastrophic declaration to increase the amount of federal assistance provided for the incident. If that became the case, a catastrophic declaration would incentivize requests for the declaration and drive up the costs of federal funding for disaster relief.

Natural disasters on a truly catastrophic scale, such as the San Francisco earthquake and fire of 1906 and Hurricane Katrina, are infrequent, and might be called "100-year events." If used for such events the declaration might not be put to use for an extended period of time. If a catastrophic declaration is used infrequently, it might become antiquated over time and fail to meet the needs of the incident. Furthermore, infrequent use of the declaration could create confusion because lawmakers and officials may have to become reacquainted with the declaration before applying its provisions. Thus, it could be argued that these incidents would be better handled through special legislation on an as-needed basis.

Potential Alternatives to a Catastrophic Declaration

Perhaps the strongest rationale for the development of a catastrophic declaration grew out of the Hurricane Katrina response and recovery experience which began in 2005 and now, nearly six years later, is still the focus of debate and the template for legislative attempts aimed at improving response and recovery.

While considering the possible changes and improvements that could potentially be a part of a catastrophic declaration, reviewing the changes that have been made since the Katrina disaster could be useful.

The Post-Katrina Act made some significant changes to the Stafford Act. Since the changes were not retroactive and could not be applied to the Katrina disaster, the actual program adjustments have not been fully tested. These changes include

- *The authority to provide case management for disaster victims.*[37] This change provides assistance for a major disaster where large numbers of people may be displaced and need help in understanding the assistance that is available, and to connect people, particularly those with special needs, with other forms of help from both public and private sources.

- *Removal of the $5,000 cap on home repairs to make a home habitable.*[38] Under the Disaster Mitigation Act of 2000, home repairs were limited to $5,000 with the remainder of work to be accomplished with a Small Business Administration disaster loan, assuming an applicant qualified for the loan. Since the Post-Katrina Act, repairs can be done for up to the maximum amount available under the Individuals and Households Program (IHP).[39]

- Pilot *Program for Public Assistance (PA).* The PA pilot program accelerated debris removal at the local level by permitting payment of straight time wages to government employees involved in debris removal work and encouraged local communities to have a debris removal plan in place by decreasing the state and local share by 5% of costs (from 25% to 20%).[40] This authority expired in 2008. FEMA intends to develop regulations to implement provisions of the PA pilot. This would include a public comment period and related parts of the rule-making process. While FEMA considers this "a priority of the Agency" it has not yet determined a timeframe for publication of the proposed rule.[41]

- Pilot Program for Individual Assistance (IA). This pilot program permitted FEMA to make repairs on privately owned rental units to increase the available housing stock after a disaster event.[42] Reports by FEMA indicate that this was a successful program that decreased temporary housing costs in comparison to other housing alternatives. The authority for the program expired on December 31, 2008. As with the PA Pilot, FEMA released a report two years ago on the IHP pilot program. The report concluded that "Analysis and recommendations on additional authorities will be provided at a later date."[43] FEMA now has determined that "through our existing authority, that we may repair multi-family rental housing units for use by disaster survivors. We expect to implement this authority in future disasters, as appropriate."[44]

Taken together, these changes to Stafford created a more flexible framework that can more easily be scaled up to meet the needs of extraordinary events. However, as the discussion of adding a catastrophic declaration attests, there is considerable debate concerning whether additional changes are necessary to increase FEMA's ability to assist state and local governments and individuals and families affected by disasters.

APPENDIX. SOURCES

1871 Chicago Fire
Wayne Blanchard, Ph.D., Worst Disasters - Lives Lost (U.S.), Federal Emergency Management
Agency, FEMA Emergency Management Higher Education Project, July 5, 2006.

1900 Galveston Hurricane
National Oceanic and Atmospheric Administration, The Great Galveston Hurricane of 1900, August 30, 2007, http://celebrating200years.noaa.gov/ magazine/ galv_ hurricane/.

1906 San Francisco Earthquake
Wayne Blanchard, Ph.D., Worst Disasters - Lives Lost (U.S.), Federal Emergency Management
Agency, FEMA Emergency Management Higher Education Project, July 5, 2006.

1919 Influenza Pandemic
Wayne Blanchard, Ph.D., Worst Disasters - Lives Lost (U.S.), Federal Emergency Management
Agency, FEMA Emergency Management Higher Education Project, July 5, 2006.

1929 Great Mississippi Flood
Hydrologic Information Center, Flood Losses: Compilation of Flood Loss Statistics, National Oceanic and Atmospheric Administration/National Weather Service, Silver Spring, MD, February 1, 2011.

1964 Alaska Earthquake/Tsunami
United States Geological Survey, 40th Anniversary of "Good Friday" Earthquake Offers New Opportunities for Public and Building Safety Partnerships, Reston, VA, March 26, 2004, http://www.usgs.gov/newsroom/ article.asp?ID=106.

1969 Hurricane Camille
National Oceanic and Atmospheric Administration /National Weather Service, Hurricane Camille 1969, Flowood, MS, August 20, 2010, http://www.srh.noaa.gov/jan/?n=*1969 08 17 hurricane camille.*

Edward N. Rappaport , Jose Fernandez-Partagas, and Jack Beven, The Deadliest Atlantic Tropical Cyclones, 1492 - Present, APPENDIX 1: Atlantic tropical cyclones causing at least 25 deaths, April 22, 1997, http://www.nhc.noaa.gov/pastdeadlya1.html.

1974 Xenia (Easter) Tornado Outbreak
National Oceanic and Atmospheric Administration, Weather Service Commemorates Nation's Worst Tornado Outbreak, March 31, 1999, http://www. publicaffairs.noaa.gov/storms/release.html.

1978 Love Canal
Eckardt C. Beck, The Love Canal Tragedy, Environmental Protection Agency, January 1979, http://www.epa.gov/history.

2008 Hurricane Ike
Robbie Berg, Tropical Cyclone Report: Hurricane Ike, National Hurricane Center, AL092008, May 3, 2010, p. 9, http://www.nhc.noaa.gov/pdf/TCR-AL092008_Ike_3May10.pdf.

1980 Mount St. Helens
Robert I. Tilling, Lyn Topinka, and Donald A. Swanson, Economic Impact of the May 18, 1980 Eruption, United States Geological Survey, Eruptions of Mount St. Helens: Past, Present, and Future: USGS Special Interest Publication, 1990.

1989 Loma Prieta Earthquake
Robert A. Page, Peter H. Stauffer, and James W. Hendley II, Progress Toward A Safer Future Since the 1989 Loma Prieta Earthquake, United States Geological Survey, U.S. Geological Survey Fact Sheet 151-99 Online Version 1.0, 1999, http://pubs.usgs.gov/fs/1999/fs151-99/.

1992 Hurricane Andrew
National Oceanic and Atmospheric Administration, Famous Hurricanes of the 20th and 21st Century In the United States 1900 - 2004, September 16, 2010.

1995 Chicago Heat Wave
Jim Angel, The 1995 Heat Wave in Chicago, Illinois, Illinois State Climatologist Office, Champaign, IL, http://www.isws.illinois.edu/atmos/ statecli/General/1995Chicago.htm.

1989 Hurricane Hugo
National Oceanic and Atmospheric Administration, Famous Hurricanes of the 20th and 21st Century In the United States 1900 - 2004, September 16, 2010.

1994 Northridge Earthquake
United States Geological Survey, Alaska and Washington Yield Largest U.S. Earthquakes ... Most Significant Earthquakes of '96 Rattle China, Indonesia, February 13, 1997, http://www.usgs.gov/newsroom/article_ pf.asp? ID=975.

2001 September 11th Terrorist Attacks
National Commission on Terrorist Attacks Upon The United States, 9/11 Commission Report, Notes On Chapter 9, Washington, DC, p. 552.

2005 Hurricane Katrina
Richard D. Knabb, Jamie R. Rhome, and Daniel P. Brown, Tropical Cyclone Report, National Oceanic and Atmospheric Administration/National Hurricane Center, Hurricane Katrina 23-30 August 2005, August 9, 2006, p. 11, http://www.nhc.noaa.gov/pdf/TCR-AL122005_Katrina.pdf.

2008 Hurricane Ike
National Oceanic and Atmospheric Administration/National Hurricane Center, Hurricane History: Ike 2008, http://www.nhc.noaa.gov/ HAW2/english/history.shtml#ike.

ARkStorm Scenario
United States Geological Survey, Overview Of The ARkStorm Scenario, Open File Report 2010-1312, http://pubs.usgs.gov/of/2010/1312/of2010-1312_text.pdf.

New Madrid Earthquake

U.S. Congress, House Committee on Science and Technology, Subcommittee on Technology and Innovation, The Reauthorization of the National Earthquake Hazards Reduction Program: R&D for Disaster Resilient Communities, Hearing, 111th Congress, June 11, 2009.

South San Andreas Fault Earthquake

U.S. Congress, House Committee on Science and Technology, Subcommittee on Technology and Innovation, The Reauthorization of the National Earthquake Hazards Reduction Program: R&D for Disaster Resilient Communities, Hearing, 111th Congress, June 11, 2009.

End Notes

[1] For example see Richard T. Sylves, "President Bush and Hurricane Katrina: A Presidential Leadership Study," *Annals of the American Academy of Political and Social Science*, volume 604 (March 2006), pp. 26-56, U.S. Congress, Senate Committee on Homeland Security and Governmental Affairs, *Hurricane Katrina: A Nation Still Unprepared*, 109th Cong., 2nd sess., S.Rept. 109-322 (Washington: GPO, 2006); U.S. Congress, House Select Bipartisan Committee to Investigate the Preparation for and Response to Hurricane Katrina, *A Failure of Initiative: Final Report of the House Select Bipartisan Committee to Investigate the Preparation for and Response to Hurricane Katrina*, 109th Cong., 2nd sess., H.Rept. 109-377 (Washington: GPO, 2006), and the White House Homeland Security Council, *The Federal Response to Hurricane Katrina: Lessons Learned* (Washington: February 23, 2006).

[2] For example, see U.S. Congress, House Committee on Transportation and Infrastructure, Subcommittee on Economic Development, Public Buildings and Emergency Management, *Post Katrina: What it Takes to Cut the Bureaucracy and Assure a More Rapid Response After a Catastrophic Disaster*, Opening Statement of Representative Diaz-Balart, 110th Cong., 1st sess., July 27, 2009.

[3] Frances Townsend, *The Federal Response to Hurricane Katrina: Lessons Learned*, The White House, Washington DC, February 23, 2006, p. 52, http://library.stmarytx.edu/acadlib/edocs/katrinawh.pdf.

[4] P.L. 93-288, 42 U.S.C. 5721 et seq.

[5] Historic events that might qualify for a catastrophic declaration are the 1906 San Francisco earthquake and fire, the terrorist attacks of September 11, 2001, and Hurricane Katrina. A catastrophic declaration might be used for a nuclear bomb explosion, a tsunami hitting a highly populated area, or an immense and destructive earthquake, among others.

[6] For further analysis on the Stafford Act see CRS Report RL33053, *Federal Stafford Act Disaster Assistance: Presidential Declarations, Eligible Activities, and Funding*, by Francis X. McCarthy.

[7] For more information on emergency and disaster declarations see CRS Report RL34146, *FEMA's Disaster Declaration Process: A Primer*, by Francis X. McCarthy.

[8] For example, the Red Cross. In some cases FEMA will assign services from other federal agencies. These are called "Mission Assignments."

[9] P.L. 93-288, 42 U.S.C. Sec. 5191(b). Examples of these declarations include the April 19, 1995 bombing of the Alfred P. Murrah Building in Oklahoma City, and the September 11, 2001 attack on the Pentagon.

[10] 44 CFR 204.24.

[11] P.L. 93-288, 42 U.S.C. Sec. 5187(a).

[12] P.L. 93-288, 42 U.S.C. Sec. 5122(1).

[13] For additional information on the differences between major disaster and emergency declarations, see CRS Report RL33053, *Federal Stafford Act Disaster Assistance: Presidential Declarations, Eligible Activities, and Funding*, by Francis X. McCarthy.

[14] Recent examples of pre-event declarations include emergency declarations prior to Hurricanes Katrina, Rita, and Gustav making landfall (emergency declarations 3212, 3260, and 3290 respectively).

[15] P.L. 93-288, 42 U.S.C. Sec. 5122(2).

[16] Mitchell L. Moss and Charles Shellhamer, *The Stafford Act and Priorities for Reform*, The Center for Catastrophe Preparedness & Response, New York University, p. 14.

[17] P.L. 109-295, Department of Homeland Security Appropriations Act, 2007. 120 STAT. 1395-1463.

[18] 6 U.S.C. 701(4).

[19] The NRF is the United States' core emergency and disaster response document. The Catastrophic Incident Annex is a companion document explicating response activities in the event of a catastrophic incident such as a large hurricane. For further analysis on the NRF, see CRS Report RL34758, *The National Response Framework: Overview and Possible Issues for Congress*, by Bruce R. Lindsay.

[20] 44 CFR 206.35(d).

[21] Federal Emergency Management Agency, *Catastrophic Incident Annex*, Washington DC, November 2008, p. 2, http://www.fema.gov/pdf/emergency/nrf/nrf_ CatastrophicIncident Annex.pdf.

[22] P.L. 109-295, Sec. 602, 120 STAT. 1395(15). The Post-Katrina Act defines surge capacity as "the ability to rapidly and substantially increase the provision of search and rescue capabilities, food, water, medicine, shelter and housing, medical care, evacuation capacity, staffing (including disaster assistance employees), and other resources necessary to save lives and protect property during a catastrophic incident."

[23] There are 15 ESFs and seven Incident Annexes. See http://www.fema.gov/emergency/nrf/ mainindex.htm. For further analysis on the NRF Annexes, see CRS Report RL34758, *The National Response Framework: Overview and Possible Issues for Congress*, by Bruce R. Lindsay.

[24] P.L. 93-288, 42 U.S.C. Sec. 5170b, Sec. 5172, and Sec. 5173.

[25] For additional information on the cost-share issue see CRS Report R41101, *FEMA Disaster Cost-Shares: Evolution and Analysis*, by Francis X. McCarthy.

[26] Straight-time force would provide the state funds to pay all labor costs, rather than only overtime costs. See C.F.R. Title 44—Emergency Management and Assistance.

[27] Currently capped at $5 million per community. See 44 C.F.R. 360.361(b). That cap was removed for Special Katrina loans.

[28] 42 U.S.C. 5170a and 5170b.

[29] The 1919 Influenza Pandemic is included in *Table 2* but is not included the analysis because the incident skews the results. See "Caveats and Methodology".

[30] As part of an economic analysis required by Executive Order 12866, the issuing agencies often place the monetary value on expected health benefits by determining the number of "statistical lives" that the rules are expected to extend or save, and then multiplying that number by an estimated "value of a statistical life." For further analysis on how agencies monetize statistical lives see CRS Report R41140, *How Agencies Monetize "Statistical Lives" Expected to Be Saved By Regulations*, by Curtis W. Copeland.

[31] For example, in terms of damages alone, the 1871 Chicago Fire was the costliest disaster in the United States ($168 billion). Thus, to determine the 90th percentile the following formula was used: $168,000,000,000 \times 0.90 = $151,200,000,000$. The formula for the 80th percentile was: $168,000,000,000 \times 0.80 = $134,400,000,000$, and so on.

[32] Excluding the 1919 Influenza Pandemic as an outlier.

[33] Methodology: $400,000,000,000 \times 0.90 = $360,000,000,000$, $400,000,000,000 \times 0.50 = $200,000,000,000$, and $400,000,000,000 \times 0.40 = $160,000,000,000$.

[34] Methodology: $630,000,000,000 \times 0.90 = $567,000,000,000$, $630,000,000,000 \times 0.60 = $378,000,000,000$, and $630,000,000,000 \times 0.10 = $63,000,000,000$. The 1919 Influenza Pandemic is included in *Table 2* but is not included in the analyses because the incident skewed the results. See "Caveats and Methodology."

[35] The ARkStorm is a hypothetical study conducted by the USGS that combines prehistoric flood history in California with modern flood mapping and climate-change projections to produce a hypothetical but, according to the USGS, plausible disaster scenario. See http://pubs.usgs.gov/of/2010/1312/ for an overview of the scenario.

[36] For similar problems regarding the role of the Federal Coordinating Officer (FCO) and the Principal Federal Official (PFO), see CRS Report RL34758, *The National Response Framework: Overview and Possible Issues for Congress*, by Bruce R. Lindsay.

[37] 42 U.S.C. 5189d.

[38] P.L. 109-295, 120 Stat. 1448.

[39] Originally set at $25,000, with Consumer Price Index adjustments, the total amount available to households under IHP is now in the $30,000 range. SBA loans can be for up to $200,000 for the repair of primary homes.

[40] P.L. 109-295, 120 Stat. 1455.

[41] E-mail to the author from Ted Litty, Senior Policy Advisor, Response and Recovery, Federal Emergency Management Agency, Department of Homeland Security, May 18, 2011.

[42] P.L. 109-295, 120 Stat. 1454.

[43] U.S. Department of Homeland Security, Federal Emergency Management Agency, *Individuals and Households Pilot Program*, Fiscal Year 2009 Report to Congress, May 19, 2009, p. 15.

[44] E-mail to the author from Ted Litty, Senior Policy Advisor, Recovery Division, Federal Emergency Management Agency, Department of Homeland Security, May 18, 2011.

In: The Catastrophic Declaration Proposal...   ISBN: 978-1-61942-264-3
Editors: Landon West and Adrian Porter © 2012 Nova Science Publishers, Inc

Chapter 2

FEDERAL STAFFORD ACT DISASTER ASSISTANCE: PRESIDENTIAL DECLARATIONS, ELIGIBLE ACTIVITIES, AND FUNDING[*]

Francis X. McCarthy

SUMMARY

The Robert T. Stafford Disaster Relief and Emergency Assistance Act (the Stafford Act) authorizes the President to issue major disaster or emergency declarations in response to catastrophes in the United States that overwhelm state and local governments. Such declarations result in the distribution of a wide range of federal aid to individuals and families, certain nonprofit organizations, and public agencies. Congress appropriates money to the Disaster Relief Fund (DRF), through both annual appropriations and emergency supplemental appropriations, for disaster assistance authorized by the Stafford Act. The Federal Emergency Management Agency (FEMA) within the Department of Homeland Security (DHS) administers most, but not all, of the authority the statute vests in the President.

The most recent significant action concerning the statute occurred in the closing months of the 109th Congress as a result of the congressional

---

[*] This is an edited, reformatted and augmented version of a Congressional Research Service publication, CRS Report for Congress RL33053, from www.crs.gov, dated June 7, 2011.

investigation on the response to Hurricane Katrina (August 2005). Senators inserted Stafford Act amendments into the FY2007 DHS appropriations legislation (Title VI of P.L. 109-295). These amendments expanded FEMA's authority to expedite emergency assistance to stricken areas, imposed new planning and preparedness requirements on federal administrators, provided new authority to regional offices, and increased federal assistance to victims and communities. More recently, Congress included a provision in the FY2010 appropriations legislation (P.L. 111-83) that allows retired law judges to arbitrate conflicts concerning the recovery of public infrastructure in the Gulf Coast due to Hurricanes Katrina and Rita. While not an amendment to the Stafford Act, this provision affects the administration of the FEMA appeals process under which applications for Stafford assistance are reconsidered. The decisions made to date by the arbitration panels resulted in an Administration request for supplemental funding that resulted in P.L. 111-112, which added more than $5.5 billion to the Disaster Relief Fund.

Previously introduced legislation during the 111th Congress would have amended the statute. Among the proposals, H.R. 3377, the Disaster Response, Recovery, and Mitigation Enhancement Act of 2009, would have authorized the Disaster Relief Fund, provided health benefits to temporary or intermittent federal employees who provide disaster assistance, authorized the National Urban Search and Rescue Response System, and requested FEMA to update standards for individual assistance disaster requests. Other bills sought to reauthorize a mortgage and rental assistance program terminated in 2000 (H.R. 888/S. 763), establish new eligibility criteria (H.R. 941, H.R. 1059, H.R. 1494, H.R. 2484, H.R. 4141, and S. 1069), and mandate establishment of a tracking and storage plan for housing units used by disaster survivors (H.R. 3437/S. 713).

OVERVIEW OF THE STAFFORD ACT

The Robert T. Stafford Disaster Relief and Emergency Assistance Act (the Stafford Act) authorizes the President to issue major disaster, emergency, and fire management declarations, which in turn enable federal agencies to provide assistance to state and local governments overwhelmed by catastrophes.[1] The statute also authorizes the President to determine whether certain types of authorized assistance will be provided and the conditions under which the aid is distributed.

The Stafford Act comprises the following titles:

- Title I: findings, declarations, and definitions;
- Title II: preparedness and pre-disaster mitigation authority;
- Title III: administrative provisions;
- Title IV: major disaster assistance;
- Title V: emergency assistance;
- Title VI: emergency preparedness (previously the Civil Defense Act of 1950);
- Title VII: miscellaneous provisions.

Titles IV and V identify the types of assistance that may be provided, and, in some circumstances, the limitations on the aid.[2] Most of the presidential authority set out in Titles IV and V in the statute, with the exception of the authority to issue declarations, has been delegated to administration officials— currently the Secretary of the Department of Homeland Security (DHS)— through executive orders.[3] Following the investigation into the response to Hurricane Katrina, Congress also authorized the Administrator to provide federal leadership before and after catastrophes, including "assisting the President in carrying out the functions" of the Stafford Act.[4]

Stafford Act definitions establish eligibility for assistance and the conditions that may be catalysts for presidential action. The definition of "major disaster" is relatively restrictive — "any natural catastrophe" including storms, earth movements and high water, and "regardless of cause, any fire, flood or explosion."[5] Presidents Bush and Obama issued 55 major disaster declarations in calendar year 2009.[6] By comparison, the definition of "emergency" is broad, authorizing the President to determine "any occasion or instance" when federal aid is needed by state and local governments to save lives and property or to address the threat of a catastrophe. In calendar year 2009, President Bush issued one emergency declaration for the presidential inauguration in the District of Columbia; President Obama issued six others in the remainder of the year, five for winter storms and one for a refinery explosion in Puerto Rico.[7] The statute also authorizes the President to provide fire suppression assistance to prevent a forest or grassland fire from becoming a major disaster.[8] President Obama issued 48 fire management declarations in 2009; President Bush issued one before leaving office, for a yearly total of 49 such declarations.[9]

Stafford Act assistance funding derives from appropriations made to the Disaster Relief Fund (DRF), administered by DHS.[10] Federal assistance supported by the DRF, and authorized in Title IV (for major disasters) or Title

V (for emergencies) provides grants for mass care for disaster survivors, the restoration of damaged or destroyed facilities, amelioration of the impact of future disasters, clearance of debris, and aid for those with uninsured critical needs. The statute also authorizes loans to communities that suffer significant revenue losses as a result of major disasters.[11] In addition, the statute authorizes unemployment assistance directly related to the event (administered by the Department of Labor) and allows federal agency heads to provide technical assistance, personnel, equipment and other resources to help state and local response and recovery efforts.

While the President may exercise discretion under authority of the statute, that authority is circumscribed by the act's administrative provisions. Federal aid cannot duplicate that provided by other sources. Federal agency heads may waive administrative, but not statutory, requirements to expedite assistance. A federal coordinating officer, appointed by the President (or the designee), ensures that federal and non-federal assistance provided to major disaster or emergency areas is coordinated. Applicants for aid must purchase appropriate levels of insurance. Title III of the statute sets out these and other administrative requirements and limitations.

The 1974 Disaster Relief Act, as Amended

The Stafford Act consists of the text of the statute enacted by Congress in 1974 and that of a series of amendments approved over the past 35 years that have added administrative requirements, enhanced the types of assistance that may be provided, expanded eligibility to certain non-profit organizations, and coordinated Stafford assistance with other federal authorities.[12]

The act maintains a two-part orientation first established in a 1950 statute (superseded by the 1974 legislation), as follows: (1) federal assistance supplements state and local relief and recovery efforts and, (2) is triggered only by a presidential declaration that is preceded by a gubernatorial request for assistance.[13]

The scope of the statute has expanded considerably over the decades to provide a wide range of grants for the needs of individuals, families, certain community organizations, and state and local government operations. The congressional investigation initiated to address questions about the response to Hurricane Katrina, which struck in August 2005, culminated in enactment of amendments that established new levels of assistance, but perhaps more importantly, addressed administrative concerns. The following section highlights the more significant amendments adopted in 2006.

The 2006 Amendments

Through the Post-Katrina Emergency Management Reform Act of 2006 (Title VI, P.L. 109-295) and, to a lesser extent, the Security and Accountability for Every Port Act of 2005, known as the SAFE Port Act (P.L. 109-347), Congress expanded the authority of FEMA to provide assistance and imposed requirements on federal officials to ensure that effective pre-disaster preparation actions would be taken.[14] Assistance for service animals and pets, pre-disaster authority, evacuation planning, and individual case management are some of the enhancements included in these amendments. While augmenting federal assistance authorities such as these, the amendments maintained state, local, and individual emergency management responsibility and accountability. In short, the Post-Katrina Act expanded the President's federal disaster assistance authority, but left the basic tenets of the Stafford Act (such as Presidential discretion, need for state requests, most restrictions on eligibility) unchanged.

The changes to the Stafford Act enacted by Congress in 2006 may be summarized as follows:

- Expedited federal assistance. The President is now authorized to support precautionary evacuation measures, accelerate federal emergency response and recovery aid, and provide expedited federal assistance (coordinated with the state to the extent possible) in the absence of a specific request from state officials.[15]
- Aid to individuals with special needs. Disabled individuals now receive federal housing assistance on sites that meet their needs, "whenever practicable," with the inclusion in the Stafford Act of the definition of "individual with a disability" from the Americans With Disabilities Act of 1990.16 Also, durable medical equipment, such as that needed by the disabled, may be provided,17 and the FEMA Administrator must develop guidelines concerning the accommodation of individuals with disabilities with regard to emergency facilities and equipment.[18] The amendments also prohibit discrimination toward the disabled, those with special needs, and those with limited proficiency in the English language.[19] To assist the latter segment of disaster victims, the FEMA Administrator must ensure that information is made available to those with limited

English proficiency, and must develop and maintain information on model language assistance as well as best practices for the state and local governments working with these individuals.[20] Also, the Pets Evacuation and Transportation Standards Act of 2006 authorizes grants to states for the improvement of emergency shelters to accommodate pets and service animals.[21]

- *Expanded assistance to disaster victims.* The President is authorized to provide transportation assistance to those displaced from their residences, including aid needed to move among alternative temporary shelters or to return to their original residence. The President may also provide case management services to state, local, or qualified private organizations that provide assistance to victims.[22]

- *Housing assistance.* Seven provisions in the 2006 amendments expanded the scope of federal housing assistance to be made available to victims.[23] First, in order to be considered eligible for housing assistance, victims of major disasters or emergencies who are disabled must be unable to access or inhabit their homes.[24] Prior to enactment of the 2006 amendments the statute did not differentiate disabled access from that experienced by other disaster victims. Second, alternative housing sites provided to victims by the federal government must meet physical accessibility requirements.[25] Third, the amendments eliminated the statutory ceilings on financial aid to be provided for housing repair and replacement,[26] but did not eliminate the overall cap of $25,000 that may be provided to each individual or household under Section 408.[27] Fourth, the amendments authorize the President to provide semi-permanent housing where no alternatives exist.[28] Fifth, the statute includes as newly eligible housing-assistance costs both utility costs (excluding telephone service) and security deposits.[29] Sixth, the disposal of temporary housing units (generally referred to as "FEMA trailers") is to be coordinated with the Department of the Interior or other federal agencies to facilitate the transfer of the units to tribal governments.[30] Seventh, the amendments established a demonstration project, the Individuals and Households Pilot Program, to increase the use of existing rental housing to provide temporary housing for victims of major disasters. Through the pilot program, which expired December 31, 2008, the Administrator was to provide for the repair and improvement of multi-family rental properties in disaster areas to increase the rental stock available to disaster victims in the immediate area.[31]

- *Public assistance (PA) to state and local governments.* State or local governments or eligible private nonprofit-facility owners may apply for federal assistance to build a new facility in a different location if all parties determine that a damaged facility should not be repaired or replaced. Such assistance, known as the "in-lieu" contribution (a grant made in-lieu of replacing or repairing a facility that existed before the disaster), has been authorized since 1974 and consists of PA grants based on the federal estimate of the cost of repair or replacement.[32] The 2006 amendment in the SAFE Ports Act deleted the clause that authorized an in-lieu grant for 90% of the federal share of the estimate of repairing or replacing the facility solely in areas with unstable soil. Now all stricken state and local governments, not just those in areas marked by unstable soil, may apply for a 90% in-lieu grant.[33] The SAFE Ports Act also authorized expedited payments for debris removal to state or local governments or to owners of qualified private nonprofit facilities.[34] In addition, the SAFE Ports Act amended the Community Disaster Loan (CDL) provisions by authorizing loans to local governments (capped at $5 million) that, because of a major disaster, suffer significant losses in tax revenue.[35] Another PA change required the President, through the FEMA Administrator, to conduct a pilot program of incentives for local and state government involvement in debris removal and the acceleration of repair work.[36]

- *Assistance to nonprofit organizations.* Three significant changes were adopted regarding the federal aid provided to private nonprofit organizations affected by a major disaster. First, the statute authorizes the President, within stated constraints, to define facilities that provide "essential services of a governmental nature to the general public."[37] These provisions, similar to those in FEMA regulations, establish eligibility for museums, zoos, performing arts facilities, community arts centers, and other facilities that "provide health and safety services of a governmental nature" as long as they provide "essential services of a governmental nature to the general public," as defined by the President.[38] Third, the amendments added the word "education" to the listing in the section of the law that defines critical services. Through this change, private nonprofit education organizations may apply directly for a FEMA grant without having to apply for a Small Business Administration loan.[39]

- *Hazard mitigation.* Section 404 of the Stafford Act authorizes the Hazard Mitigation Grant Program (HMGP) for grants to states in which major disasters have been declared.[40] These funds must be used for activities that prevent future disasters or reduce their impact if they cannot be prevented. The Post-Katrina Act adjusted the percentage amounts for HMGP awards by establishing a scale that authorizes a higher percentage (15% of the total Stafford Act assistance in a state) for major disasters in which no more than $2 billion is provided, 10% for assistance that ranges from more than $2 billion to $10 billion, and 7.5% for major disasters that involve Stafford Act assistance of more than $10 billion to $35.3 billion.[41]

- *Administrative changes.* The 2006 amendments authorize the President to appoint one Federal Coordinating Officer (FCO) for a multi-state event, in addition to deputy FCO's as needed.[42] Traditionally, one FCO has been named for each separate disaster declaration in each respective state. The statute also amends the Stafford Act by requiring that the President designate a Small State and Rural Advocate in FEMA to ensure that rural community needs are met in the declaration process and to help small states prepare declaration requests, among other duties.[43] Other administrative changes concern the authority and capabilities of organizations charged with the response to the major disaster site. The amendments authorize the President to establish at least three national response teams and others as deemed necessary (including regional response teams), and require that FEMA team members possess essential capabilities, training skills, and equipment.[44] In addition, the SAFE Ports Act amended the Stafford Act by adding a new definition, "essential service providers," defined as persons affiliated with municipal governments or private entities who will help restore essential services to a stricken area. Such workers are not to be impeded when they seek access to a disaster site.[45]

Action in the 111th Congress

Legislation introduced in the 111th Congress could have expanded categories of federal assistance in the Stafford Act and, if enacted, make relatively minor adjustments to the statute. Selected examples of the legislation and summaries of the policy changes that would be incorporated into the statute are listed below:

- *H.R. 888 and S. 763:* Temporary mortgage and rental assistance would be authorized for victims in areas included in a major disaster declaration. Congress previously authorized the assistance from 1974 until enactment of the 2000 amendments which vitiated the provision as part of the efforts by the 106th Congress and the Clinton Administration to constrain federal emergency management costs.

- *H.R. 941 and S. 1069:* H.R. 941 would designate owners or operators of a private or investor-owned electric utility company serving low-income households to be eligible for grants for the repair or replacement of damaged facilities. S. 1069 would do the same for owners or operators of investor owned energy facilities, under certain conditions. As explained later in this report (see "Expanding Eligibility" section) this issue has been debated in the past as certain utilities that provide public services have no recourse to Stafford assistance.

- *H.R. 1239:* States could apply for grants to establish revolving loan funds to enable homeowners and businesses to undertake hazard mitigation activities. This legislation would amend the pre-disaster mitigation authority (Section 203 of the act). Experience gained under the mitigation efforts funded through a pilot program established through the Bunning-Bereuter-Blumenauer Flood Insurance Reform Act of 2004 for severe repetitive loss properties in flood plains may be applicable to congressional consideration of this proposal.[46]

- *S. 713 and H.R. 3437*: These two bills would modify existing disaster housing provisions. If enacted, H.R. 3437 would mandate that the FEMA Administrator develop lifecycle plans and tracking procedures for mobile housing units provided to individuals and households. Units found to be hazardous to the occupants' health would be repaired before being used for disaster-related housing needs.[47] Similarly, but not as an amendment to the Stafford Act, S. 713 would mandate that the FEMA Administrator evaluate the existing stock of temporary housing units and plan for their disposition or storage.

- *H.R. 3466:* The President would be authorized to consolidate funds for public infrastructure restoration for disasters involving "extensive and widespread damage and destruction" with no cost share required from state or local governments.[48]

- *S. 764:* The ceiling on the amount to be available for individual and household assistance for lower income residents in states with high costs of living would be increased to a base of $50,000, from $25,000, to be adjusted annual for inflation.

- *H.R. 3377*: A number of changes would be made to the Stafford Act through this legislation. Funding would be authorized through FY2012 for the Pre-Disaster Mitigation program (described below in this report), the Administrator of FEMA would be required to modernize and modify the existing federal public warning and alert system, the Mortgage and Rental Assistance program would be reauthorized, temporary or intermittent employees who provide disaster assistance would be eligible for federal health benefits, the National Urban Search and Rescue Response system would be authorized, the Disaster Relief Fund would be authorized, and grants for hazard mitigation would be increased if states meet minimum building code standards.[49]

Enacted Legislation

While no amendments to the Stafford Act were enacted in the 111th Congress, two public laws should be noted for the measures they include that affect administration of the statute. First, provisions in a supplemental appropriations statute for FY2009 authorized the FEMA Administrator to extend the payment for case management programs related to Hurricanes Katrina and Rita and mandated a 90/10 cost share for public assistance stemming from Hurricane Ike, storms in Kentucky and Kansas, among other purposes.[50] Second, the FY2010 appropriations statute for DHS authorizes the reemployment of retired administrative law judges to settle disputes related to the arbitration panels established in the American Recovery and Reinvestment Act of 2009 in order to expedite recovery from Hurricanes Katrina and Rita. This change in procedure is discussed at the end of this report, see "Appeal Process" section, below.[51]

OVERVIEW OF STAFFORD ACT DECLARATIONS

Major disaster and emergency declarations are two of the five types of actions that may be taken under authority of the Stafford Act.[52] The other three include fire management declarations, the provision of defense resources before a major disaster is declared, and the decision to pre-position supplies and resources.[53]

Prior to a Disaster

Three types of declarations (or commitments) may be made under Stafford Act authority before a catastrophe occurs. First, at the request of a governor, the President may direct the Department of Defense (DOD) to commit resources for emergency work essential to preserve life and property in "the immediate aftermath of an incident" that may result in the declaration of a major disaster or emergency (discussed below).[54] The statute does not define the term "incident." According to regulations, upon receiving a gubernatorial request for such assistance, the FEMA Associate Director may determine that DOD aid is necessary to save lives and protect property.[55]

Second, the Stafford Act authorizes the President to provide fire management assistance in the form of grants, equipment, personnel, and supplies to supplement the resources of communities when fires on public property or on private forests or grasslands threaten destruction that might warrant a major disaster declaration.[56] Implementation of this authority, which has been delegated to FEMA officials, requires that a gubernatorial request be submitted while an uncontrolled fire is burning. To be approved, state applications must demonstrate that either of the two cost thresholds established by FEMA through regulations has been reached.[57] The thresholds involve calculations of the cost of an individual fire or those associated with all of the fires (declared and non-declared) in a state each calendar year.[58] FEMA officials determine whether a fire management assistance declaration will be issued.[59]

Third, when a situation threatens human health and safety, and a disaster is imminent but not yet declared, the Secretary of DHS may pre-position employees and supplies. DHS monitors the status of the situation, communicates with state emergency officials on potential assistance requirements, deploys teams and resources to maximize the speed and effectiveness of the anticipated federal response and, when necessary, performs preparedness and preliminary damage assessment activities. A related provision enacted in 2006 authorizes the FEMA Administrator to provide evacuation preparedness assistance to non-federal officials.[60]

After receiving a request from the governor of an affected state for a major disaster declaration, the President may take one of three possible actions: issue a major disaster declaration or an emergency declaration, or decline the request.[62]

After a Catastrophe Occurs

The Stafford Act authorizes the President to issue two types of declarations—major disaster and emergency—after an incident overwhelms state and local resources.[61]

Major Disaster Declarations

Major disaster declarations may be issued after a natural catastrophe "(including any hurricane, tornado, storm, high water, wind-driven water, tidal wave, tsunami, earthquake, volcanic eruption, landslide, mudslide, snowstorm, or drought)" or, "regardless of cause, [after a] fire, flood or explosion."[63]

Regulations further specify the factors considered by FEMA in evaluating a gubernatorial request for a major disaster declaration. The factors considered to determine whether federal PA assistance is needed include an assessment of the per capita impact of the disaster within affected states;[64] insurance coverage in force; the presence and impact of hazard mitigation measures; the cumulative impact of disasters over the previous year; and, whether federal aid authorized by statutes other than the Stafford Act would better meet the needs of stricken areas.[65] Factors considered to determine whether federal IHP assistance is needed include concentration of damages; number of injuries, deaths, or the extent to which essential services are disrupted; the impact on special populations that require higher levels of assistance; the extent to which voluntary agencies are able to meet the needs of victims; insurance coverage; and, measurements of needs such as disaster housing needs approved, number of homes destroyed or damaged, financial assistance required, and others.[66]

Emergency Declarations

The declaration process for emergencies is similar to that used for major disasters, but the criteria (based on the definition of "emergency") are less specific.[67] Whereas all major disaster declarations require a gubernatorial request and, generally, findings and certifications as summarized above, emergency declaration requirements are less rigorous. For example, the President may issue an emergency declaration without a gubernatorial request if primary responsibility rests with the federal government.[68] Also, specific thresholds or calculations of past averages are not considered, but FEMA officials do assess whether "all other resources and authorities available to meet the crisis are inadequate" before recommending that the President issue an emergency declaration.[69]

TYPES OF ASSISTANCE AND ELIGIBILITY

The Stafford Act identifies the universe of eligible applicants (e.g., states, local governments, owners of certain private nonprofit facilities, individuals, or families). However, not all persons or entities affected by a catastrophe are eligible for Stafford Act assistance even if the President issues a declaration. FEMA officials determine the need for assistance after a major disaster or emergency declaration is issued. Aid is provided only to those persons or entities determined to need the assistance. For example, a family with adequate insurance and alternative housing options might not be considered eligible to receive financial aid. A unit of local government that suffers damages to some facilities, but not to the extent considered necessary pursuant to FEMA regulations and guidelines, might not receive funds to rebuild infrastructure.

The type of assistance made available varies from one disaster to another and among eligible applicants within a state, commensurate with decisions by FEMA officials on the extent of damage and the eligibility of applicants. For instance, under a major disaster declaration, local jurisdictions with large numbers of damaged or destroyed residences might be eligible for assistance under the Individual Assistance (IA) program, whereas those with severely damaged infrastructure but relatively few damaged homes might be eligible only for assistance under the PA program. Similarly, if a local government had extensive debris in public rights-of-way due to a disaster, but very little damage to public facilities, a determination might be made to provide assistance only for debris removal activities under the PA program. On the other hand, areas severely devastated by a catastrophe are often eligible for both IA and PA.

The Stafford Act authorizes the President to make the initial determination of eligibility for federal relief and recovery assistance through the issuance of either a major disaster or emergency declaration. The following subsections summarize the types of assistance authorized under each.

Major Disaster Assistance

A major disaster declaration authorizes the President to direct that the following types of federal disaster assistance may be provided, depending upon the specific needs of the stricken areas:

- *General federal assistance* supports state and local governments in that it facilitates the distribution of consumable supplies; authorizes federal agency heads to provide resources (with or without reimbursement) to support evacuations, response and recovery efforts; and, provides a range of technical and advisory help.[70]

- *Essential assistance* authorizes federal agency heads to distribute aid to victims through state and local governments and voluntary organizations, perform life- and property-saving assistance, clear debris, and conduct search and rescue missions, among other immediate response services. (The statute also allows Governors to request the use of Department of Defense resources before a major disaster or emergency declaration is issued.)[71]

- *Hazard mitigation* grants are provided to each state in which a major disaster declaration is issued to reduce risks and damages that might occur in future disasters.[72]

- *Federal facilities* may be repaired, restored, replaced, or reconstructed, if necessary, before legislation is enacted. If necessary, such construction may be undertaken before appropriations are approved if funds can be transferred from accounts dedicated to other purposes.[73]

- *Repair, restoration, and replacement of damaged facilities* is administered through the Public Assistance (PA) program. Public facilities and infrastructure systems owned by state and local governments, as well as private nonprofit facilities that provide essential services, may be repaired or rebuilt. Applicants may also seek contributions for other facilities or hazard mitigation measures in lieu of repairing or restoring damaged facilities;[74]

- *Debris removal* may be funded through the use of federal resources or through grants to state or local governments or owners of private nonprofit facilities.[75]

- *Assistance to individuals and households* administered through the Individual and Household Program (IHP), includes financial grants to rent alternative housing, direct assistance through temporary housing units (mobile homes), and limited financial assistance for housing repairs and replacement. Financial assistance for uninsured medical, dental, funeral, personal property, transportation, and other expenses (referred to as Other Needs Assistance (ONA) is also authorized.[76]

- *Unemployment assistance* is available to individuals unemployed as a result of the major disaster, for up to 26 weeks, as long as they are not entitled to other unemployment compensation or credits.[77]
- *Grants to assist low-income migrant and seasonal farmworkers* are provided by the Secretary of Agriculture (total limited to $20 million annually) "where the Secretary determines that a local, state or national emergency or disaster" has resulted in a loss of income or inability to work.[78]
- *Food coupons and food distribution* for low-income households unable to purchase nutritious food;[79]
- food commodities for emergency mass feeding;[80]
- legal services for low-income individuals;[81]
- crisis counseling assistance and training grants for state and local governments or private mental health organizations to provide services or train workers;[82]
- community disaster loans to local governments that lose tax or other revenues needed for governmental services;[83]
- emergency communications to establish temporary communications during "or in anticipation of an emergency or major disaster,"[84] and,
- emergency public transportation to provide transportation to essential places.[85]

Each major disaster declaration specifies the type of incident covered, the time period covered, the types of disaster assistance available, the units of local government (generally counties, parishes, and independent cities) included in the declaration, and the name of the federal coordinating officer. As the effects of the catastrophe subside over time, the initial major disaster declaration may be amended to modify the types of assistance to be provided and the areas (generally counties) included in the major disaster declarations.

Emergency Declaration Assistance

Considerably less assistance is authorized to be provided under an emergency declaration in comparison to that authorized for a major disaster declaration. The types of emergency assistance authorized to be provided under an emergency declaration include the following:

- activities to support state and local emergency assistance;
- coordination of disaster relief provided by federal and non-federal organizations;
- technical and advisory assistance to state and local governments;
- emergency assistance through federal agencies;
- debris removal through grants to state and local governments (Section 407);
- grants to individuals and households for temporary housing and uninsured personal needs (Section 408); and
- distribution of medicine, food, and consumables.[86]

FUNDING CAPS AND COST SHARES

Before federal assistance is provided under Stafford Act authority contractual agreements between FEMA and the state must be finalized. These agreements set forth the terms under which FEMA will obligate and distribute disaster assistance funding to the state for redistribution to eligible applicants (e.g., local governments).

Pursuant to Stafford Act requirements, federal assistance programs are limited either to a fixed dollar amount or to a percentage of eligible costs. All parties use the agreements to establish federal, state, and local cost shares pursuant to statutory requirements and allowances. The Stafford Act stipulates that the minimum federal assistance for certain eligible activities "shall be not less than 75% of the eligible cost of such assistance."[87] Other provisions specify ceilings, rather than floors, for federal aid. Specific cost share requirements set out in the statute include the following.

- *Essential assistance:* The federal share must be at least 75% of eligible costs.[88]
- *Repair, restoration, or replacement of public facilities*: In general, at least 75% of eligible costs must be provided, but this threshold may be reduced to 25% if a facility has previously been damaged by the same type of disaster and mitigation measures have not been adopted to address the hazard. Federal aid generally will be reduced if facilities in flood hazard areas are not covered by flood insurance. Cost estimation requirements must be adhered to, but the President may approve costs that exceed the regulatory limitations. "Associated

costs," such as the employment of national guard forces, use of prison labor, and base and overtime wages for employees and "extra hires," may be reimbursed. The President must notify congressional committees with jurisdiction before providing more than $20 million to repair, restore, or replace facilities.[89]

- *Debris removal*: The federal share must be at least 75% of the eligible costs.[90]

- *Individual and household assistance:* Temporary housing units may be provided directly to victims of disasters, without charge, for up to 18 months, unless the President extends the assistance "due to extraordinary circumstances." Fair market rents may be charged at the conclusion of the 18 month period.[91] The federal share of housing assistance is 100%. Financial assistance is also provided for Other Needs Assistance (ONA). This includes uninsured medical, dental, funeral, transportation, personal property, and other needs; the federal share for ONA is capped at 75% of eligible costs; the total amount that may be provided under the Individuals and Household Program (IHP) cannot exceed $25,000 (adjusted annually).[92]

- *Small project grants:* If the estimated costs of assistance for facility repair or replacement (Section 406), essential assistance (Section 403), debris removal (Section 407), or emergency assistance (Section 502) do not exceed $35,000 (adjusted annually), a small project grant may be issued.[93]

- *Emergency declaration assistance:* Federal assistance must constitute at least 75% of eligible costs. Expenditures made under an emergency declaration are limited to $5 million per declaration unless the President determines that there is a continuing need; Congress must be notified if the $5 million ceiling is breached.[94]

In instances where the state-local match is unduly burdensome due to factors such as the impact of the disaster or the fiscal condition of the state and its units of local government, the President may waive some or all of the cost-sharing requirement for PA programs. However, the President may not waive the 25% state-local requirement for assistance provided under the Individual Assistance (IA) Program, except for insular areas.[95] As noted previously in this report, Congress statutorily waived the cost share provision for assistance provided after specified disasters.[96]

If a state or a local government believes that the economic impact from the disaster warrants, officials may contact FEMA to request a reduction in their portion of the federal cost-share. The regulations specify that an adjustment in the cost-share requirement may be made "whenever a disaster is so extraordinary that actual federal obligations under the Stafford Act, excluding FEMA administration cost, meet or exceed" specified thresholds.[97] (The costs incurred are based on Stafford Act obligations for the disaster and may differ from those of the preliminary damage assessment.[98])

HAZARD MITIGATION ASSISTANCE

Under the Hazard Mitigation Program Grant (Section 404 or HMGP) and the Pre-Disaster Mitigation grant (Section 203 or PDM) authorities the federal government provides grants to state and local governments to reduce the impact of future disasters.[99] HMGP funds are allocated to each state in which a major disaster has been declared. The funds generally may be used for any eligible hazard mitigation activity in the state (consistent with the Governor's request and Presidential designation), not necessarily related to the catastrophe that led to the declaration. PDM grants, by comparison, are applied for pursuant to criteria established in Section 203 and are not related to major disaster declarations.

Section 404 Hazard Mitigation Grants

HMGP funding was first authorized in the 1988 amendments to the 1974 statute.[100] Congress has amended Section 404 four times since 1988 to (1) increase the share of federal assistance and authorize property acquisition grants,[101] (2) stimulate state mitigation planning,[102] (3) reduce the maximum amount of federal aid,[103] and (4) establish a sliding scale for the awards.[104] Money for HMGP derives from the Disaster Relief Fund (DRF, discussed in the next section of this report), not from line item appropriations. The current statutory provisions do not address what percentage would be used to determine hazard mitigation funding for disasters that exceed $35.333 billion. It would appear that special legislation would need to be enacted to provide mitigation funding for any disaster in excess of that amount.

Pre-Disaster Mitigation Grants

During the Clinton Administration FEMA initiated a new program titled Project Impact to stimulate pre-disaster mitigation efforts.[105] Congress appropriated funds, generally $25 million per year, in the mid-1990s, to support Project Impact activities. The 105th Congress considered, but did not approve, legislation to authorize funding for pre-disaster mitigation grants.[106] The issue carried over to the 106th Congress, which approved legislation to expand federal pre-disaster mitigation assistance in order to reduce federal disaster relief costs, save lives, and protect property through enactment of the DMA of 2000.[107]

The pre-disaster mitigation (PDM) grant program established by the DMA is intended to reduce losses and suffering "resulting from natural disasters" and provide a source of funding to ensure "the continued functionality of critical services and facilities after a natural disaster."[108] Assistance is authorized to help state and local governments implement "pre-disaster hazard mitigation measures that are cost-effective and are designed to reduce injuries, loss of life, and damage and destruction of property, including damage to critical services and facilities under the jurisdiction of the states or local governments."[109] Successful applicants must demonstrate the ability to develop "effective public-private natural disaster hazard mitigation partnerships. The legislation, according to FEMA, "emphasizes the importance of strong state and local planning processes and comprehensive program management at the state level."[110] Funding appropriated for PDM grants remains available until expended.[111]

DISASTER RELIEF FUND

Congress appropriates money to the Disaster Relief Fund (DRF) to ensure that the federal assistance described earlier in this report is available to help individuals and communities stricken by severe disasters.[112] Funds appropriated to the DRF remain available until expended. Such accounts are referred to as "no-year" accounts.[113] Appropriations to the DRF generally evoke little controversy. Supplemental appropriations measures are generally required each fiscal year to meet the urgent needs of particularly catastrophic disasters. While the hurricane season of 2009 (June through October) resulted in no major disaster declarations for named hurricanes, 56 severe storms during calendar year 2009 caused a level of destruction sufficient for the

President to invoke Stafford authority.[114] In addition to the appropriation of $1.6 billion in regular appropriations for FY2010 to meet the needs associated with those and previous declarations, the fund also received an additional $5.5 billion through P.L. 111-112, based on a request from the Obama Administration for supplemental funding for FY2010 to pay for Gulf Coast recovery projects that have been the subject of decisions by an arbitration panel established pursuant to a congressional mandate.. The "Appeal Process" section at the end of this report discusses the impact of the panel's actions on the appropriation of supplemental FY2010 funds for the DRF.

Questions have been raised in the past concerning the increased cost of federal disaster assistance authorized by the Stafford Act as the categories of aid and eligibility for federal disaster assistance have expanded. For example, over the past five decades, Congress has expanded the basic authority first enacted in 1950 to include housing, grants for the repair of infrastructure, aid to individuals, loans to communities for lost revenue, and other needs. Congress has previously explored the issue of rising federal disaster assistance costs and reliance upon supplemental appropriations.[115] See "Reducing Federal Expenditures," for a discussion of this topic.

Mission Assignments

The DRF is the source of funding for "mission assignments" made by FEMA to other federal agencies. By this mechanism the federal government is able to provide assistance after a disaster by tasking any federal agency to undertake an activity necessary to save lives, protect property, or provide other assistance authorized by the Stafford Act. Mission assignments eliminate the need for Congress to appropriate specific amounts of money to many federal agencies. Instead, this instrument enables FEMA to task and reimburse other federal agencies for the assistance they undertake after the President issues a declaration.

For example, FEMA's Operation Blue Roof, the program that funds the installation of blue tarps to temporarily repair damaged residential roofs, is mission assigned to the U.S. Army Corps of Engineers (USACE). The Corps of Engineers obtains and distributes the tarps, hires the contractors, and ensures that all applicable federal regulations are followed. Other activities that may fall under FEMA mission assignments to other federal agencies include search and rescue, disease prevention and control, and health and medical support.

ISSUES FOR THE 112TH CONGRESS

As noted above, previously introduced legislation would amend provisions of the Stafford Act concerning eligibility for assistance, the types of assistance to be provided by the federal government, and administration of the emergency management process. Members of the 112th Congress might elect to consider the following in assessing whether further legislative changes are required.

Expanding Eligibility

The 1988 amendments to the Disaster Relief Act of 1974 added certain private nonprofit organizations that provide essential government services to the category of eligible recipients of Stafford Act public assistance.[116] Prior to that change, only state and local governments were eligible for the aid. Legislation introduced during the 111th Congress suggested further changes to the Stafford Act by enabling certain organizations or persons to receive assistance for which they are not currently eligible.

The most significant proposals would breach the long-standing bright line that has divided public and for-profit entities. Private for-profit organizations and property owners have not been deemed eligible for grants authorized by the statute since enactment of the 1950 statute and in subsequent amendments. Instead, Congress has directed that owners and operators of private, for-profit institutions must rely on pre-paid insurance or loans. The devastation caused by Hurricane Katrina to all components of many communities, and the recognition that community recovery is tied not only to public institutions but to private sector entities that provide essential services and employment, has revived interest in the issue of expanding eligibility for Stafford Act assistance to certain for-profit entities.

In addition to adding new organizations to the category of entities eligible for public assistance, some have suggested that the Congress take a different approach to extending Stafford Act assistance. Currently, only property owners are eligible to receive financial assistance for the repair or replacement of housing, some of the legislation from the 111th Congress sought to make several changes:

- H.R. 1059 would extend eligibility to the heirs of deceased property owners. Another approach is to modify the definition of the term "major disaster" to include other types of catastrophes.
- H.R. 1131 would authorize the President to issue such a declaration after instances of terrorist attacks, contamination, or most broadly, "or other catastrophic event."[117]
- Other bills (H.R. 3377 and H.R. 3453) would take a different approach; they would require that Administration officials revise and update the criteria currently used to determine whether a major disaster declaration will be issued.
- Also, one bill (H.R. 4297) would require that the President consider the needs of rural areas marked by less dense land development in determining eligibility for assistance. Revisions to the criteria for declarations could result in expanded eligibility for aid, or, as discussed below, possibly lead to reduced federal expenditures.

Some might contend that any such expansion of eligibility would result in considerably higher federal disaster relief expenditures as private, for-profit entities, newly designated property owners, or entire states would increasingly turn to federal grants in lieu of relying upon insurance policies or agreeing to repay loans. Accordingly, opponents of the proposals might argue that just as the 2000 amendments expanded certain federal assistance (largely through the establishment of a new pre-disaster hazard mitigation program) and reduced costs in some areas, the pending legislation should balance increased aid proposals with cost-cutting measures.[118]

Others would contend that amendments that would expand the boundaries of eligibility are appropriate as state and local governments struggle with budget problems, property owners face increased costs of credit, and policyholders face more expensive insurance premiums and more stringent insurance requirements. Also, they may contend that just as some of the facilities newly designated as eligible for public assistance funds in 1988, notably educational and health care institutions, provide services comparable to those available through public or non-profit organizations, the institutions identified in the pending legislation also provide public services critical to a community's revival. Such a conclusion, it might be argued, is consistent with congressional findings in the statute.[119]

As discussed below, precedent exists for the provision of such assistance. On at least two occasions, Congress appropriated funds to help private corporations deemed to be particularly affected after disasters—when utility companies' electricity lines were damaged in 1998 ice storms, and when other companies lost infrastructure in the terrorist attacks of 2001 in New York City. A third instance, involving the Texas Medical Center, directly involves Stafford Act eligibility criteria. The first two instances involved appropriations made outside of Stafford Act authority, the third consisted of special designation under the Stafford definition.

Private Utilities after the 1998 Ice Storms

In the early winter months of 1998, an ice storm resulted in the destruction of electricity distribution infrastructure as heavily laden trees collapsed on miles of poles and wires.[120] Private utilities owned and maintained the infrastructure. To address concerns that the private utilities would have to pass on the costs of repairs to customers, Congress included funding in the omnibus appropriations act for FY1999 (P.L. 105-277) for the Community Development Block Grant (CDBG) program administered by the Department of Housing and Urban Development (HUD). The act directed that funds would be provided "for disaster relief, long-term recovery, and mitigation in communities affected by Presidentially-declared natural disasters designated during fiscal years 1998 and 1999."[121] According to news reports, disagreement arose between the Secretary of HUD and Members of Congress over the use of the appropriated funds because the statute did not specify how the funds would be used.[122]

Private Utilities after the 2001 Terrorist Attacks

The destruction of much of the infrastructure around and under the World Trade Center on September 11, 2001, resulted in the appropriation of billions of dollars in federal assistance to New York City. The communications networks owned by private for-profit corporations were not eligible for assistance under the Stafford Act. Congress appropriated $783 million for a range of rebuilding efforts in Lower Manhattan, for economic revitalization and reconstruction in order to facilitate redevelopment, "including the restoration of utility infrastructure."[123] The conference report accompanying the legislation provided the following statements regarding this appropriation:

> The conference agreement includes an emergency appropriation of $783,000,000 for assistance to properties and businesses, including restoration of damaged infrastructure, and for economic revitalization activities in the areas of New York City affected by the September 11, 2001

terrorist attacks, instead of $750,000,000 as proposed by the House and Senate.

The conferees recognize the tremendous human losses suffered by those businesses located in the World Trade Center, particularly those firms which suffered the greatest loss of life in the attacks. Because of the conferees' strong desire to support the redevelopment of the areas of New York City affected by the attacks and to encourage those businesses most devastated by the attacks to remain in New York City, the conferees have provided a $33,000,000 increase over the request. The conferees expect that these additional funds will be made available to assist those firms located in New York City at the time of the terrorist attacks which suffered a disproportionate loss of its workforce and who intend to re-establish their operations in New York City.

The conferees concur with the language included in the House report encouraging the Lower Manhattan Development Corporation to consider the needs of utility companies and other institutions affected by the World Trade Center attacks.[124]

Private Health System after 2001 Tropical Storm Allison

In early June, 2001, President Bush issued a major disaster declaration for the state of Texas due to flooding associated with Tropical Storm Allison.[125] The Texas Medical Center (TMC), a health care complex that includes 13 hospitals as well as medical and nursing schools, suffered considerable damage.[126] The TMC, however, was not eligible for Stafford Act assistance because of its for-profit status. Through a provision included in an omnibus appropriations statute, TMC was declared eligible for Stafford Act assistance, as follows:

> That notwithstanding any other provision of law, for disaster declaration FEMA-1379-DR and hereafter, the Texas Medical Center is to be considered for FEMA Public Assistance and Hazard Mitigation grants as if it were an eligible applicant.[127]

Policy Options

Members of Congress might elect to take action on or in opposition to the legislation noted above in order to expand eligibility for Stafford Act assistance. Another option available to Members of Congress is to consider the integration of existing loan authority with the grant-in-aid provisions in the Stafford Act. Congress already moved in this direction in 2000 with the requirement that public assistance grants be available to certain non-profit facilities "only if" they provide critical services (defined in the statute) or the owner or operator has applied for a Small Business Administration (SBA) loan and has been found ineligible for such aid or has received the maximum amount of assistance possible through such a loan.[128] Congress might elect to consider modifying the thresholds for assistance by authorizing grants for businesses before they obtain loans at the maximum level or eliminating the requirement that they be found ineligible for such aid. One research organization cited the need for a legislative change such as this as follows:

> Currently, there are no federal grants programs — only loans — to assist small business. We further recommend converting some federal assistance for small businesses from loans to grants in order to ease the burden of loan repayments following a catastrophe. The amount of grants versus loans could be weighted depending upon the size and history of the business.[129]

The integration of the SBA disaster loan authority and the Stafford Act grant-in-aid assistance authority has previously been considered by Congress decades ago. First, when President Richard Nixon proposed the establishment of a Department of Community Development, the integration of "the disaster relief programs of the SBA and the Farmers Home Administration" were expected to be integrated with the transfer of emergency preparedness and disaster relief functions.[130] Congress did not act on President Nixon's proposal. Next, when President Jimmy Carter successfully reorganized federal emergency management authorities in 1978 through the creation of FEMA, the loan-making authority and resources of the SBA were viewed as separate activities from those moving into FEMA. In questioning Administration officials on the Carter proposal, one Senator argued for the separation of FEMA's coordination authority from the SBA loan authority as follows:

> I would think that, first of all, we would have for the first time in the government a single accountable public official with broad coordinative authority over all disaster relief programs. We are not going to be duplicating staffs in agencies such as the Farmers' Home Administration or Small Business Administration, who are very expert in making loans and following up and managing loans. But we are going to have a place in the government where overall policies can be developed ... I think we will be able to address overall emergency related policies, including those of programs that are actually carried out by other agencies.[131]

Members of the 112th Congress might elect to reopen the debate on whether loan authority, including that currently administered by the SBA, might be recast to address concerns raised in the discussion on whether Stafford act grant-in-aid eligibility might be expanded.

Reducing Federal Expenditures

The need for federal assistance after a disaster, particularly one of catastrophic magnitude, may lead some Members and other officials to promise "whatever it takes" to restore the area to its pre-disaster condition. The knowledge that families have been disrupted, livelihoods compromised, and basic governance threatened stimulate congressional action to ensure that past precedents are followed and, at times, additional aid is provided. Such assistance, however, requires the expenditure of revenues that might arguably be used elsewhere for other urgent purposes. For years Congress has wrestled with the competing goals of providing disaster assistance and controlling expenditures. The debate, often muted in the face of devastating losses, continues today.

In light of the ongoing discussions in the 112th Congress to reduce the federal deficit and federal expenditures, Members of Congress may wish to consider changes to the Stafford Act that would reduce federal expenditures. One of the most straightforward, and arguably difficult options, is to eliminate or reduce some of the benefits authorized by the statute. That option would require an examination of the components of the Stafford Act, their relative costs, and the effect of enacting changes to current benefits.[132] Should Members elect to consider other options, they may wish to consider past efforts to reduce expenditures.

Perhaps the most extensive effort to evaluate the range of federal disaster assistance programs and identify alternative financing approaches involved a Senate bipartisan task force. Following the high costs associated with Hurricane Andrew in 1992, Senators formed the Bipartisan Task Force on Funding Disaster Relief to compile information on federal policies and programs, identify costs, and discuss budgetary options. The final report issued by the Task Force included a discussion of one proposal to modify disaster assistance policies: establish more explicit and/or stringent criteria for providing federal disaster assistance.[133]

Criteria for Assistance Declarations

The Senate Bipartisan Task Force report focused on the criteria considered by the President in deciding whether a major disaster or emergency declaration would be issued. The policy that currently guides the decision process is set out in statute and regulations, and provides for discretionary judgment as well.[134] As some analysts have concluded, however, the criteria have not always been well documented or consistent.

Legislation introduced in the 111th Congress (H.R. 3377 and H.R. 3453) would have mandated updating of the existing regulatory criteria used to determine whether major disaster declaration assistance (and what type of assistance) is to be provided. Such an examination may lead to the tightening of requirements that could result in reduced federal expenditures. Conversely, less stringent requirements would result in expanded eligibility and assistance levels.

The issue of which criteria are used by the President to issue a declaration has been the focus of some analytical studies. Questions have been raised about whether federal aid is needed at all after some catastrophes. Some have contended that political considerations, as much as estimates of need, contribute to the costs of disaster relief as well. One 2002 study by economists Thomas A. Garrett and Russell S. Sobel purported: "States politically important to the president have a higher rate of disaster declaration by the president, and disaster expenditures are higher in states having congressional representation on FEMA oversight committees. Election year impacts are also found." Another study, which built upon the 2002 paper, examined presidential disaster declarations from 1981 through 2004 and found that "... the greater the electoral prize and the more competitive the statewide presidential contest, the more likely it is that a state will receive a presidential disaster declaration even after controlling for actual need."[135] Another, earlier perspective on the issue appeared in a 1989 study completed by Government Accountability Office (GAO) that also considered the effects of politics on disaster declarations. After examining presidential declaration data from the perspective of the party affiliation of governors and members of state congressional delegations, the authors concluded that there "were no indications that party affiliation affected White House major disaster declaration decisions."[136]

Members of Congress may elect to consider amending the Stafford Act to reduce the discretion exercised by the President in issuing the declarations. Such amendments might include establishing quantitative measures of need, damage thresholds higher than those currently used, or mandating that such declarations be subject to congressional review.

Individual and Family Eligibility

Stafford Act assistance for individuals (and the assistance authorized under the predecessor legislation since 1950) has never been means tested. All residents of areas included in major disaster or emergency declarations remain eligible for assistance, providing the President (through administrative officers) determine that the assistance is to be provided. Disaster survivors must provide an indication of need and assurance that federal aid will not be duplicative, but they do not have to meet income or other requirements.[137] It is arguable that the destruction of paper records and the need for victims to evacuate an area with scant or no proof of their income or other means of support, overwhelms any argument for means testing.

However, one piece of legislation introduced in the 111th Congress would have established increased individual and household assistance for disaster victims with annual incomes below $100,000. One might argue that if federal officials could obtain this information to assess the needs of lower income households for more assistance, similar information could be used to identify those with higher incomes in order to establish a maximum threshold for assistance.

In the face of record deficits and calls to reduce federal spending, Members of Congress may elect to evaluate the advantages and disadvantages of enacting a means test before housing or other needs assistance (referred to as ONA) are to be provided pursuant to Section 408 of the Stafford Act. Some may argue that means testing should not be used after a disaster when the full extent of losses is unknown, seemingly wealthy households will face new expenses, and administrative workloads will increase. Others may contend that such thresholds would result in lower federal expenditures, be consistent with the existing provision that federal aid not duplicative assistance from other sources, and encourage individuals and families to allocate personal resources to unanticipated needs.

Appeal Process

The most significant action taken by the 111th Congress regarding Stafford Act policy involved the authority of the U.S. Civilian Board of Contract Appeals to finalize decisions on public assistance applications. The FY2010 appropriations legislation for the Department of Homeland Security authorized the temporary reemployment of retired administrative law judges to preside over arbitration proceedings involving disputes of public assistance applications that exceed $500,000 in total costs.[138] Through this legislation Congress sought to expedite action on public assistance applications in the Gulf Coast that have been pending for years in order to stimulate recovery efforts in Louisiana, Alabama, Mississippi, and Texas associated with Hurricanes Katrina and Rita in 2005. Implementing regulations issued by FEMA outline the standard appeal process and summarize the conditions under which cases in appeal would be subject to the process established by Congress. [139]

From December 2009 through March 3, 2010, the Civilian Board of Contract Appeals issued 14 rulings on disputed applications.[140] The first five decisions set out the scope of the panel's authority.[141] Of the remaining nine decisions, one resulted in FEMA's favor (CBCA 1760),due to the lack of timeliness of the appeal, while seven were decided in favor of the appellants. The parties reached settlement in one decision (numbered CBCA 1781), obviating the need for a panel decision. Perhaps the most significant decision made during this period involved the disposition of Charity Hospital in New Orleans. In short, the panel ruled in favor of the appellants, and determined that FEMA should award almost $475 million for the replacement of the hospital (CBCA 1741).

Impact of Panel Decisions on Funding

The decisions to date by the appeals panel have influenced the debate between the Administration and Congress on appropriations for the DRF. Administration officials determined that the funds appropriated for FY2010 were insufficient for the Fund, in part due to the decision involving Charity Hospital and the expectation that other appeals will also result in increased demands for DRF assistance. On February 12, 2010, the President submitted a second supplemental FY2010 budget request for an additional $1.5 billion for the DRF, in addition to the $3.6 billion supplemental included in the FY2011 submission to Congress. This total supplemental of $5.1 billion, according to the Administration, would be expected to meet needs in the current fiscal year, including "arbitration panel decisions likely to impact the Disaster Relief Fund in a previously unexpected manner."[142] After Senate defeat on March 9, 2010 of a proposal to include the supplemental in legislation (H.R. 4123) that would extend expiring tax provisions, Members of Congress eventually passed the supplemental to the Disaster Relief Fund in P.L. 111-112 that provided more than $5.5 billion in additional supplemental disaster relief funding.

Summary of Issues on Appeals Process

While limited to appeals of decisions associated with Hurricanes Katrina and Rita, the congressional action indicates some degree of dissatisfaction with the standard appeals process established through regulation under the broad statutory guidance in the Stafford Act.[143] As opined by a former General Counsel for FEMA, the decision by Congress to authorize the arbitration process reflects "congressional belief that the appeal process for FEMA's public assistance program was broken ...."[144]

The issue before Congress is whether the appeal process requires a "fix," and whether that modification should take the form of a statutory change.

The regulations issued by FEMA implementing the arbitration process identified the criteria to be considered in determining whether public assistance applications could be submitted to the arbitration process as follows: large projects that exceed the $500,000 statutory threshold, applicants who remained eligible to file an appeal under the standing regulations (44 CFR 206.206) and withdrew their appeal, and those applicants that met specified time frames and deadlines. The regulation vested final determinative authority with the majority of arbitration panel members.[145] According to the statement accompanying the final rule, approximately 44 appeals were pending in Mississippi and Alabama (Hurricane Katrina), Texas (Hurricane Rita) and Louisiana (both hurricanes) when the agency published the regulation. Also, 2,188 projects were awaiting initial rulings and were estimated to be subject to the process. Accordingly, FEMA expected that 127 appeals would be forthcoming out of the 2,188 large projects eligible for the arbitration process [146] The actual number of appeals submitted to arbitration, however, are far below the estimate. According to the former General Counsel for FEMA, "More than a dozen applicants have elected arbitration ...."[147]

At least three topics may be explored by Members of Congress if they elect to debate the need for a statutory change.

- First, would an arbitration panel or other determinative party outside of FEMA be designated to participate in the appeals process, or should appeals continue to be heard and decided upon solely by FEMA administrators? It may be argued that only FEMA officials are most familiar with the details of public assistance grants, the application requirements, and comparable applications.[148] The cost estimates, circumstances unique to that particular disaster (such as the availability of skilled contractors and material), need for modifying initial damage projections, and other factors arguably require considerable knowledge of the public assistance grant program.149 Others may contend that this familiarity of the process and ownership of required information complicates efforts by appellants to even determine whether they should seek arbitration or appeal a FEMA decision, and may not meet the statutory mandate that rules "provide for the fair and impartial consideration of appeals under this section."150 For example, the quality of information available to appellants may be questioned, as summarized by the former FEMA General Counsel, "The rules assume that an applicant has the information and documentation required to establish eligibility at the outset of the arbitration process.... In fact, FEMA frequently is the only party with information that allows applicants to understand and respond to the disallowance of cost in an appeal (or an arbitration). And FEMA's responsiveness to FOIA [Freedom of Information Act] requests is notoriously slow — generally requiring a number of months.151 One option that Members might consider involves enacting an amendment that would mandate that FEMA maintain and provide applicable information to the appellants within the time frame established for an applicant deciding to file an appeal. Another option would maintain the current appeals process but provide for a final determinative authority outside of FEMA, perhaps through the permanent establishment of an arbitration panel comparable to that established by the 111th Congress, through the Federal Arbitration Association, or an arbitrator assigned to the matter through the Federal Arbitration Act (9 U.S.C. 1 et seq.)

- Second, the arbitration panel established pursuant to the American Recovery and Reinvestment Act of 2009 is solely authorized to consider appeals related to the Stafford Act public assistance program. As noted previously in this report, assistance is also provided to individuals and households for housing and uninsured needs, and the statute provides for appeal regulations that address decisions related to any assistance provided under the authority of Title IV.

- There is no provision for public review or consideration of the arbitration panel process. Congress might elect to consider whether the proceedings should remain closed.

End Notes

[1] The Robert T. Stafford Disaster Relief and Emergency Assistance Act, 42 U.S.C. 5121 et seq. "States" include U.S. territories and the District of Columbia. In addition to the assistance authorized by the Stafford Act, a wide range of disaster aid is provided by other federal agencies under statutory authority that specifically refers to disaster assistance, as well as under general assistance provisions. For information on the range of federal programs see CRS Report RL31734, *Federal Disaster Recovery Programs: Brief Summaries*, by Carolyn V. Torsell.

[2] See "Types of Assistance and Eligibility" in this report for information on the categories of aid available under Stafford Act authority.

[3] U.S. President George W. Bush, "Amendment of Executive Orders, and Other Actions, in Connection with the Transfer of Certain Functions to the Secretary of Homeland Security," E.O. 13286, Sec. 52, February 28, 2003.

[4] The authority of the FEMA Administrator to assist the President were incorporated into the Homeland Security Act, as amended by P.L. 109-295, 120 Stat. 1398 (6 U.S.C. 314(8)).

[5] 42 U.S.C. 5122(2).

[6] President Bush issued declarations in January 2009 before President Obama took office. For information on declarations see "2009 Federal Disaster Declarations," at http://www.fema. gov/news/disasters.fema?year=2009. For information on the declaration process see CRS Report RL34146, *FEMA's Disaster Declaration Process: A Primer*, by Francis X. McCarthy.

[7] Ibid.

[8] 42 U.S.C. 5187.

[9] See http://www.fema.gov/news/disasters.fema?year=2009.

[10] For current appropriations information see CRS Report R40642, *Homeland Security Department: FY2010 Appropriations*, coordinated by Jennifer E. Lake. For historical information see CRS Report R40708, *Disaster Relief Funding and Emergency Supplemental Appropriations*, by Bruce R. Lindsay and Justin Murray.

[11] Congress appropriates funds for the community disaster loan program separate from the DRF.

[12] The Disaster Relief Act of 1974 was enacted in P.L. 93-288, 88 Stat 143 et seq. The 1988 amendments (P.L. 100-707, 102 Stat. 4689 et seq.), which retitled the 1974 statute to its current designation, constituted the most far reaching amendments until those enacted in 2006 in the Post-Katrina Emergency Management Reform Act (P.L. 109-295, 120 Stat. 1444-1457. In addition, the Disaster Mitigation Act of 2000 (P.L. 106-390, 114 Stat. 1552 et seq. established some cost cutting requirements and authorized a new hazard mitigation program. For a history of the evolution of the statute and federal emergency management as a policy area see Rubin, Claire, ed. *Emergency Management; The American Experience, 1900-2005*, Public Entity Risk Institute (http://www.riskinstitute.org), 2007.

[13] The untitled 1950 statute is P.L. 81-875, 64 Stat. 1109-1111.

[14] In addition to amending the Stafford Act, the Post-Katrina Emergency Management Reform Act amended the Homeland Security Act to expand the authority of the Administrator of FEMA and the mission of the agency. See P.L. 109-295, 120 Stat. 1395-1406.

[15] P.L. 109-295, §681, 120 Stat. 1444, which amended Sec. 402 and 502 of the Stafford Act.

[16] P.L. 109-295, §688(3), which amended Sec. 102, 120 Stat. 1448 of the Stafford Act. See housing assistance at 42 U.S.C. 5174(d)(1)(A).

[17] P.L. 109-295, §689(b), which amended Sec. 403, 120 Stat. 1449 of the Stafford Act.

[18] P.L. 109-295, § 689(a), 120 Stat. 1448-1449. For more information see CRS Report RS22254, *The Americans with Disabilities Act and Emergency Preparedness and Response*, by Nancy Lee Jones.

[19] P.L. 109-295, §689a, 120 Stat. 1449.

[20] P.L. 109-295, §689e, new Stafford Act Sec. 616, 120 Stat. 1452. Note that Sec. 616 refers to the FEMA "Director," not Administrator, the title created in the 2006 amendments.

[21] P.L. 109-308, Sec. 3, Stafford Act amended Sec. 611, 120 Stat. 1725.

[22] P.L. 109-295, §689f, new Stafford Act Sec. 425 and Sec. 426, 120 Stat. 1452-1453. Note that the SAFE Ports Act also added a new Sec. 425 to the Stafford Act ("Essential Service Providers"), codified at 42 U.S.C. 4189e.

[23] For information on federal disaster housing assistance see CRS Report R40810, *FEMA Disaster Housing: From Sheltering to Permanent Housing*, by Francis X. McCarthy.

[24] P.L. 109-295, §689(c), Stafford Act amended Sec. 408, 120 Stat. 1449.

[25] P.L. 109-295, §689(c), Stafford Act amended Sec. 408, 120 Stat. 1449.

[26] P.L. 109-295, §686, Stafford Act amended Sec. 408(c), 120 Stat. 1448.

[27] The Stafford Act provides for annual cost of living adjustments to the funding ceiling. Effective October 1, 2006, the maximum amount that may be provided to an individual or household under the IHP authority is $28,800. See 71 *Federal Register* 59514.

[28] P.L. 109-295, §685, Stafford Act amended Sec. 408(c), 120 Stat. 1447.

[29] P.L. 109-295, §689d, Stafford Act amended Sec. 408, 120 Stat. 1452.

[30] P.L. 109-295, §689k, 120 Stat. 1456.

[31] P.L. 109-295, § 689i, 120 Stat. 1454. Following the Midwest floods in May of 2008 the state of Iowa made use of the pilot program, as did Texas following Hurricane Ike in the fall of 2008. FEMA has indicated it believes it has sufficient authority within the Stafford Act to continue this pilot program when needed.

[32] P.L. 93-288, 88 Stat. 154, amended by P.L. 100-707, 102 Stat. 4699. In 1988 Congress reduced the in-lieu grant from 90% to 75% of the federal estimate and retained the 90% level solely for areas with unstable soil (P.L. 106-390, 114 Stat. 1563).

[33] P.L. 109-347, §609, Stafford Act amended Sec. 406, 120 Stat. 1942.

[34] P.L. 109-347, §610, Stafford Act amended Sec. 407, 120 Stat. 1942-1943.

[35] P.L. 109-347, §608, 120 Stat. 1942.

[36] P.L. 109-295, §689j, 120 Stat. 1455. The statute terminated the program in December 2008. FEMA has expressed its intention to incorporate some of the PA pilot program through the rule-making process.

[37] P.L. 109-295, § 688(1), Stafford Act amended Sec. 102(9), 120 Stat. 1448.

[38] Ibid. The regulations are found at 44 CFR §206.221(e)(7).

[39] P.L. 109-295, § 689h, Stafford Act amended Sec. 406, 120 Stat. 1453.

[40] 42 U.S.C. 5170c.

[41] P.L. 109-295, §684, Stafford Act amended Sec. 404, 120 Stat. 1447.

[42] P.L. 109-295, §687, Stafford Act amended Sec. 302, 120 Stat. 1448.

[43] P.L. 109-295, §689g, new Stafford Act Sec. 326, 120 Stat. 1453.

[44] P.L. 109-295, §633, Stafford Act amended Sec. 303, 120 Stat. 1421. Note that the statute refers to the "Director" of FEMA, whereas the position is identified elsewhere as "Administrator."

[45] P.L. 109-347, §607, new Stafford Act Sec. 425, 120 Stat. 1941. Note that the Post Katrina Act also added a new Sec. 425 ("Transportation Assistance") to the Stafford Act.

[46] 42 U.S.C. 4102a 47 The Chair of the Transportation and Infrastructure Committee, Representative Thompson, sponsored H.R. 3437. Mr. Thompson has reportedly asked FEMA to halt the sale of trailers to the public, citing health hazards identified in

congressional investigations. See Rob Margetta, "Experts Ponder Expanded Role for FEMA in Foreign Disasters," *CQ Homeland Security*, Jan. 14, 2010, at http://homeland.cq.com/hs/display.do?docid=3279089&sourcetype=31.

[48] This issue received attention in a hearing held during the first session of the 111th Congress. See U.S. House, Transportation and Infrastructure Committee, Subcommittee on Economic Development, Public Buildings, and Emergency Management, hearing, *Post Katrina: What it Takes to Cut the Bureaucracy*, July 27, 2009, transcript and statements at http://transportation.house.gov/hearings/hearingDetail.aspx?NewsID=960.

[49] Portions of this bill are comparable to H.R. 6658 ordered to be reported from the House Committee on Transportation and Infrastructure in the 110th Congress, but not considered by the full House nor the Senate.

[50] P.L. 111-32, 123 Stat. 1882-1883.

[51] P.L. 111-83, 123 Stat. 2185; P.L. 111-5, 123 Stat. 164.

[52] The text of the statute and pertinent regulations are presented in CRS Report RL33030, *The Budget Reconciliation Process: House and Senate Procedures*, by Robert Keith and Bill Heniff Jr. For further discussion of Stafford Act declarations, see CRS Report RL34146, *FEMA's Disaster Declaration Process: A Primer*, by Francis X. McCarthy.

[53] Whereas the first two pre-event actions are specifically authorized by the Stafford Act, the pre-event actions are inferred from general authority. Following an investigation into the response to Hurricane Andrew in 1992 the General Accounting Office (now the Government Accountability Office) reported that "Current federal law governing disaster response does not explicitly authorize federal agencies to undertake preparatory activities before a disaster declaration by the President, nor does it authorize FEMA to reimburse agencies for such preparation, even when disasters like hurricanes provide some warning that such activities will be needed." U.S. General Accounting Office, *Disaster Management: Improving the Nation's Response to Catastrophic Disasters* (Washington: July 23, 1993), p. 3.

[54] The statute reads "During the immediate aftermath of an incident which may ultimately qualify for assistance under this title or title V of this Act ... the Governor of the state in which such incident occurred may request the President to direct the Secretary of Defense to utilize the resources of the Department of Defense for the purpose of performing on public and private lands any emergency work which is made necessary by such incident and which is essential for the preservation of life and property. If the President determines that such work is essential for the preservation of life and property, the President shall grant such request to the extent the President determines practicable. Such emergency work may only be carried out for a period not to exceed 10 days." 42 U.S.C. 5170b(c).

[55] 44 CFR 206.35(c).

[56] Sec. 420 of the Stafford Act, 42 U.S.C. 5187.

[57] Regulations are found at 44 CFR 204.1 et seq.

[58] 44 CFR 204.51.

[59] 44 CFR 204.24.

[60] P.L. 109-295, §632, 120 Stat. 1421.

[61] For more information on the declaration process see CRS Report RL34146, *FEMA's Disaster Declaration Process: A Primer*, by Francis X. McCarthy.

[62] For criteria considered in the declaration of a major disaster, see 44 CFR 206.48. The gubernatorial request for a declaration is forwarded to the President through FEMA officials. Only the President may issue a major disaster declaration.

[63] 42 U.S.C. 5122(2).

[64] Each year FEMA issues a notice that identifies the threshold to be used as one factor to be considered in the determination of whether PA or IA or both will be made available after a major disaster declaration has been issued. The regulations establish a minimum threshold of $1 million in PA damages for each state; see 44 CFR 206.48(a)(1). Major disasters declared on or after October 1, 2005, would generally be expected to reach the threshold of $1.18 per capita for PA assistance to be authorized; see 70 FR 58734. However, the statewide threshold is not the sole factor. Assessments consider concentrations of damages in local jurisdictions even if statewide damages are not severe. Countywide impacts from major disasters declared on or after October 1, 2005, would generally be expected to reach the threshold of $2.94 per capita for PA assistance to be authorized; see 70 FR 58734.

[65] Citations to emergency assistance statutory authorities administered by agencies other than the Department of Homeland Security are identified in Table 2 of CRS Report RL33064, *Organization and Mission of the Emergency Preparedness and Response Directorate: Issues and Options for the 109th Congress*, by Keith Bea.

[66] Refer to the table in regulations (44 CFR 206.48(b)(6)) for computed averages of individual assistance needed for small, medium and large states, based upon losses incurred from 1994 to 1999.

[67] A Stafford Act "emergency" is "any occasion or instance for which, in the determination of the President, federal assistance is needed to supplement state and local efforts and capabilities to save lives and to protect property and public health and safety, or to lessen or avert the threat of a catastrophe in any part of the United States." 42 U.S.C. 5122(1).

[68] "The President may exercise any authority vested in him by ... this title with respect to an emergency when he determines that an emergency exists for which the primary responsibility for response rests with the United States because the emergency involves a subject area for which, under the Constitution or laws of the United States, the United States exercises exclusive or preeminent responsibility and authority. In determining whether or not such an emergency exists, the President shall consult the Governor of any affected state, if practicable. The President's determination may be made without regard to subsection (a) of this section." 42 U.S.C. 5191(b).

[69] 44 CFR 206.37(2).

[70] Sec. 402 of the Stafford Act, 42 U.S.C. 5170a.

[71] Sec. 403 of the Stafford Act, 42 U.S.C. 5170b. FEMA has established two categories of public assistance (PA) emergency work under Section 403 authority—debris removal (Category A) and emergency protective measures to save lives and property (Category B).

[72] Sec. 404 of the Stafford Act, 42 U.S.C. 5170c. The Hazard Mitigation Grant Program (HMGP), authorized by Section 404 of the Stafford Act (42 U.S.C. 5170c), funds activities that reduce the impacts of future disasters. For more information see CRS Report R40471, *FEMA's Hazard Mitigation Grant Program: Overview and Issues*, by Natalie Keegan. A second hazard mitigation program, the Pre-Disaster Mitigation (PDM) program, is authorized in Title II of the Stafford Act (42 U.S.C. 5133). For more information see CRS Report RL34537, *FEMA's Pre-Disaster Mitigation Program: Overview and Issues*, by Francis X. McCarthy and Natalie Keegan.

[73] Sec. 405 of the Stafford Act, 42 U.S.C. 5171. The statute also mandates that federal agencies evaluate and take action to mitigate natural hazards.

[74] Sec. 406 of the Stafford Act, 42 U.S.C. 5172. Private nonprofit facilities that provide "critical services" (power, water, sewer, wastewater treatment, communications, and emergency medical care) may receive grants. Owners of other facilities that provide essential, but not critical services, must first apply for a Small Business Administration (SBA) loan, and may

then receive grants if they are ineligible for such a loan or require aid above the amount approved by the SBA. The permanent work supported under this authority has been designated by FEMA as follows: "Category C," roads and bridges; "Category D," water control facilities; "Category E," buildings and equipment; "Category F," utilities; and "Category G," parks, recreational facilities, and other items. For more information see U.S. Department of Homeland Security, Federal Emergency Management Agency, "Public Assistance   Guide-FEMA   Publication   322,"   available   at http://www.fema.gov/government/grant/pa/paguided.shtm, visited August 1, 2006.

[75] Sec. 407 of the Stafford Act, 42 U.S.S. 5173. Debris removal grants authorized by Section 407 are provided to states and are separate from the Category A debris removal PA assistance authorized by Section 403.

[76] Sec. 408 of the Stafford Act, 42 U.S.C 5174. [Sec. 409, food coupons and distribution, was redesignated Sec. 412.]

[77] Sec. 410 of the Stafford Act, 42 U.S.C. 5177. For background information see CRS Report RS22022, *Disaster Unemployment Assistance (DUA)*, by Julie M. Whittaker.

[78] 42 U.S.C. 5177a.

[79] Sec. 412 of the Stafford Act, 42 U.S.C. 5179.

[80] Sec. 413 of the Stafford Act, 42 U.S.C. 5180.

[81] Sec. 415 of the Stafford Act, 42 U.S.C. 5182.

[82] Sec. 416 of the Stafford Act, 42 U.S.C. 5183.

[83] Sec. 417 of the Stafford Act, 42 U.S.C. 5184.

[84] Sec. 418 of the Stafford Act, 42 U.S.C. 5185.

[85] Sec. 419 of the Stafford Act, 42 U.S.C. 5186.

[86] Section 502 of the Stafford Act, 42 U.S.C. 5192.

[87] The Stafford Act, as amended (P.L. 100-707), Sections 403(b), 403 (c)(4), 406(b), and 407(d). The same 75% minimum is also applicable to presidential emergency declarations (42 U.S.C. 5193, Section 503(a)). Neither the statute nor the regulations impose a formula for the distribution of cost-share requirements among state and local governments. Some states, for example, have established a 15% local and a 10% state match combination; other states equally divide the required cost share—12.5% each for the state and for each local government that receives Stafford Act assistance.

[88] 42 U.S.C. 5170b(b).

[89] 42 U.S.C. 5172. The statute provides that "base and overtime wages for the employees" and hires of state and local governments may be reimbursed under this authority (42 U.S.C. 5172(a)(2)(C). Regulations, however, specify that "straight- or regular-time salaries and benefits" of permanent employees (referred to as "force account labor costs") are not eligible if they are engaged in activities associated with essential assistance (Sec. 403) or debris removal grants (Sec. 407). See 44 CFR 206.228(a)(4).

[90] 42 U.S.C. 5173(d).

[91] 42 U.S.C. 5174(c). Financial assistance to build permanent or "semi-permanent" housing may be provided in insular areas outside the continental United States "and in other locations" where temporary housing alternatives are not available.

[92] 42 U.S.C. 5174. FEMA has established a limitation of $27,200 for IHP assistance to an individual or household in each emergency or major disaster declared after October 1, 2005. See 70 FR 58735. (The 2006 amendments deleted the caps on housing repair and replacement.)

[93] 42 U.S.C. 5189. FEMA has established a limitation of $57,500 for small project grants for major disaster or emergencies declared after October 1, 2005. See 70 FR 58735.

[94] Sec. 503 of the Stafford Act, 42 U.S.C. 5193.

[95] 48 U.S.C. 1469(a)(d).

[96] P.L. 111-32, 123 Stat. 1882-1883.

[97] 44 CFR 206.47(b).

[98] Due to the difficulty of conducting preliminary damage assessments immediately after a disaster occurs, it is not unusual for amendments to be made to the disaster declaration providing more assistance to affected areas once the greater degree of damage has become known and verified. For more information, see CRS Report R41101, *FEMA Disaster Cost-Shares: Evolution and Analysis*, by Francis X. McCarthy.

[99] For more information see CRS Report R40471, *FEMA's Hazard Mitigation Grant Program: Overview and Issues*, by Natalie Keegan and CRS Report RL34537, *FEMA's Pre-Disaster Mitigation Program: Overview and Issues*, by Francis X. McCarthy and Natalie Keegan.

[100] P.L. 100-707, Sec. 106(a), 102 Stat. 4698-4699. For more information see CRS Report

[101] 1993 amendments in P.L. 103-181, §§2(a), 3, 107 Stat. 2054.

[102] 2000 amendments in P.L. 106-390, Title I, §104(a), 114 Stat. 1558.

[103] 2003 amendments in P.L. 108-7, Title IV, §417, 117 Stat. 525.

[104] 2006 amendment in P.L. 109-295, Title VI, Subtitle E, Sec. 684, 120 Stat. 1447.

[105] For background on Project Impact see U.S. Congress, House Committee on Transportation and Infrastructure, Subcommittee on Water Resources and Environment, *Disaster Mitigation, Preparedness and Response,* hearing, 105th Cong., 2nd sess., January 28, 1998 (Washington, GPO, 1988).

[106] See U.S. Congress, Senate Committee on Environment and Public Works, Subcommittee on Clean Air, Wetlands, Private Property and Nuclear Safety, *Federal Emergency Management Agency Reforms*, hearing, 105th Cong., 2nd sess., July 23, 1998 (Washington: GPO, 1999).

[107] Sec. 102, P.L. 106-290, 114 Stat. 1553-1557, 42 U.S.C. 5133.

[108] Sec. 101(b), P.L. 106-390, 42 U.S.C. 5133.

[109] 114 Stat. 1554.

[110] U.S. Federal Emergency Management Agency, "Hazard mitigation planning and Hazard Mitigation Grant Program," *Federal Register*, vol. 67, no. 38, February 26, 2002, pp.8843-54.

[111] See P.L. 108-334, the FY2005 Department of Homeland Security Appropriations Act, 118 Stat. 1313.

[112] Information on disaster funding is available in: CRS Report R40708, *Disaster Relief Funding and Emergency Supplemental Appropriations*, by Bruce R. Lindsay and Justin Murray.

[113] For background on this and other types of federal budget accounts, see CRS Report 98-410, *Basic Federal Budgeting Terminology*, by Bill Heniff Jr.

[114] The listing of declarations is found at http://www.fema.gov/news/disasters.fema?year=2009#sev1. Tropical storm/depression Ida, which did not reach hurricane status, led to declarations in two states.

[115] U.S. Congress, Senate Bipartisan Task Force on Funding Disaster Relief, *Federal Disaster Assistance*, S.Doc. 104-4, 104th Cong., 1st sess., (Washington: GPO, 1995). The House convened a task force that issued an unpublished report. Following completion of the task force efforts, some Members introduced a concurrent resolution (H.Con.Res. 39, 104th Congress) seeking a "fundamental overhaul of federal disaster policies." See also U.S. Congress, House Committee on the Budget, Task Force on Budget Process, *Budgetary Treatment of Emergencies*, hearing, 105th Cong., 2nd sess., June 23, 1998 (Washington: GPO, 1998).

[116] P.L. 100-707, 102 Stat. 4699. The 2000 amendments further modified the language concerning private nonprofit facilities by requiring that the facilities provide "critical services." See P.L. 106-390, 114 Stat. 1562.

[117] The phrase "other catastrophic event" is comparable to definitional language replaced in the 1988 amendments. From 1950 through 1988 the phrase "or other catastrophe" appeared in the definition of major disaster. (See 54 Stat. 1109 for the 1950 text.) In 1988 Congress modified the definition to more itemize the types of "natural" catastrophes that might result in a declaration and inserted "regardless of cause, any fire, flood or explosion" in place of the broader "other catastrophe" phrase (see 102 Stat. 4690 for the revised and current text).

[118] Title I of P.L. 106-390 authorized the pre-disaster mitigation program; Title II, "Streamlining and Cost Reduction," sought to reduce costs by authorizing the President to establish management cost rates, allowing states to administer their hazard mitigation (Section 404) grant programs, imposed restrictions on the awarding of grants to private nonprofit organizations, limited community development loans to $5 million, and made other changes.

[119] 42 U.S.C. 5121(b). The findings and declarations provision of the statute notes that the federal assistance is to, among other purposes, provide "programs for both public and private losses sustained in disasters." 42 U.S.C. 5121(b)(6).

[120] For background on the storm , see Senator Olympia Snowe, "The Ice Storm of 1998," remarks in the Senate, *Congressional Record*, vol. 144, February 11, 1998, S609-S612.

[121] 112 Stat. 2681-579. The full text of the provision that appropriated funds after the ice storms follows in the appendix to this memorandum.

[122] Steve Campbell, "Ice Storm Aid Pittance Seen as 'Betrayal'," *Press Herald* online, November 22, 1998, at http://www.portland.com/sunews/story2.htm, visited November 23, 1998; Charles Davant, "Congress Hastens Maine Ice Storm Relief," *Bangor Daily News*, May 12, 1999; site archived.

[123] 116 Stat. 890.

[124] U.S. Congress, Conference Committees, 2002, *Making Supplemental Appropriations for Further Recovery from and Response to Terrorist Attacks on the United States for the Fiscal Year Ending September 30, 2002, and for Other Purposes*, conference report to accompany H.R. 4775, H.Rept. 107-593, 107th Cong., 2nd sess. (Washington: GPO, 2002), p. 180.

[125] Information is available at U.S. Federal Emergency Management Agency, "Texas Severe Storms and Flooding: Declared June 9, 2001," at http://www.fema.gov/news/event. fema?id=115, visited January 28, 2008.

[126] Summary information is available at Ellen Parson, "1,000-Year Flood Paralyzes Texas Medical Center," September 1, 2002, at http://www.ecmweb.com/mag/electric_year_flood_ paralyzes/index.html, visited January 28, 2008.

[127] P.L. 108-7, 117 Stat. 514. No recorded debate exists relative to the merits of this provision.

[128] 42 U.S.C. 5172(a)(3)(A), enacted in P.L. 106-390, 114 Stat. 1562.

[129] Moss, Mitchell L. and Charles Shelhamer, New York University. *The Stafford Act: Priorities for Reform*. The Center for Catastrophe Preparedness and Response, 2007, p. 19, available at http://www.nyu.edu/ccpr/pubs/Report_StaffordActReform_MitchellMoss_10.03.07.pdf.

[130] U.S. Congress, House, Committee on Government Operations, Subcommittee on Legislation and Military Operations, *Reorganization Plan No. 1 of 1973*, hearing, Feb. 26, 1973, 93rd Cong., 1st sess., U.S. Govt. Print. Off., p. 37.

[131] U.S. Congress, Senate, Committee on Governmental Affairs, Subcommittee on Intergovernmental Relations, *Reorganization Plan No. 3 of 1978 (Disaster Preparedness)*, hearing, June 20, 1978, 95th Cong., 2nd sess., U.S. Govt. Print. Off., p. 8.

[132] Comprehensive data on federal emergency management funding are not collected on a regular basis. To the extent known, the most comprehensive collection of such data comprised expenditure information from fiscal years 1977 through 1993. A similar compilation has not been published. In constant dollars, federal disaster recovery costs totaled almost $87 billion, or slightly more than $5 million annually. The next most costly category involved hazard mitigation efforts, with a total of $27 million, or $1.6 million annually. Preparedness and response expenditures totaled less than $4 billion each for that period, or annual costs of less than $200 million. See U.S. Senate. Bipartisan Task Force on Funding Disaster Relief. *Federal Disaster Assistance, Report of the Senate Task Force on Funding Disaster Relief*, 104th Cong., 1st sess., Document No. 104-4 (Washington: GPO, 1995), Table 1.1, p. 5.

[133] U.S. Senate. Bipartisan Task Force on Funding Disaster Relief. *Federal Disaster Assistance, Report of the Senate Task Force on Funding Disaster Relief*, 104th Cong., 1st sess., Document No. 104-4 (Washington: GPO, 1995), p. 69. the report also discussed two other options: "emphasize hazard mitigation through incentives or rely more on insurance." The former is discussed earlier in this report as hazard mitigation authority exists in the Stafford Act. Greater reliance on pre-paid insurance policies raises issues beyond the scope of the Stafford Act.

[134] For information on the declaration criteria and procedures see CRS Report RL34146, *FEMA's Disaster Declaration Process: A Primer*, by Francis X. McCarthy.

[135] Andrew Reeves, "Political Disaster? Presidential Disaster Declarations and Electoral Politics," Abstract, unpublished paper, August 29, 2005, available at http://sws1.bu.edu/areeves/papers/fema.pdf.

[136] U.S. General Accounting Office, *Disaster Assistance: Timeliness and Other Issues Involving the Major Disaster Declaration Process*, GAO/RCED-89-138, May 25, 1989, pp. 1, 4.

[137] The establishment of means testing for individuals differs from the current policy used by the President and administration officials to establish criteria to determine whether declarations will be issued in states, and, if so, the considerations given to determine which counties will be included in the declaration. For information on such capacity and need measures see CRS Report RL34146, *FEMA's Disaster Declaration Process: A Primer*, by Francis X. McCarthy.

[138] The temporary reemployment authorization is found at Section 566, P.L. 111-83, 123 Stat. 218. The authorization for arbitration panels is found at Section 601, P.L. 111-5, 123 Stat. 164.

[139] U.S. Department of Homeland Security, Federal Emergency Management Agency, "Arbitration for Public Assistance Determinations Related to Hurricanes Katrina and Rita (Disasters DR-1603, DR-1604, DR-1605, DR-1606, and DR1607)," 74 *Federal Register* 44761-44769, August 31, 2009.

[140] The Board rulings are presented at http://www.cbca.gsa.gov/2009FEMA/2009FEMA.htm#October_2009.

[141] The first five rulings, found at the cite noted immediately above, are numbered CBCA 1739, 1741, 1775, 1783, and 1757.

[142] The White House, *FY2010 Supplemental Proposal in the FY2011 Budget*, p. 4 of the document found at http://www.whitehouse.gov/omb/assets/budget_ amendments/supplemental_02_12_10.pdf.

[143] Section 423 of the statute (42 U.S.C. 5189a) provides that any decision concerning Title IV (major disaster) assistance may be appealed within 60 days, requires that a decision be issued within 90 days, and that mandates that rules be issued "for the fair and impartial consideration of appeals under this section." The regulations allow eligible applicants, subgrantees, or grantees to first appeal a FEMA decision concerning an application for public assistance. Such appeals must be reviewed by grantees and then given to the FEMA regional director. If that appeal is denied, applicants may submit second round appeals to a FEMA Assistant Administrator for Disaster Assistance. The regulations set out time constraints on appellants and FEMA officials and authorize FEMA officials to, at their discretion, "submit the appeal to an independent scientific or technical person or group" with expertise in technical matters. "The decision of the FEMA official at the next higher level shall be the final administrative decision of FEMA." 44 CFR 206.206.

[144] Ernest Abbott, President, FEMA Law Associates, PLLC, *FLASH Newsletter*, vol. 4, Issue 11, April 2009, p. 1.

[145] U.S. Department of Homeland Security, Federal Emergency Management Agency, "Arbitration for Public Assistance Determinations Related to Hurricanes Katrina and Rita (Disasters DR-1603, DR-1604, DR-1605, DR-1606, and DR1607)," 74 *Federal Register* 44761-44769, August 31, 2009.

[146] The regulations note that FEMA funds slightly more than 5,000 large projects per year, and that almost 6% of those projects result in appeals. Ibid, p. 44765.

[147] Ernest Abbott, President, FEMA Law Associates, PLLC, *FLASH Newsletter*, vol. 4, Issue 13, December 2009, p. 1. Statistics on the number of projects submitted for arbitration have been requested from FEMA, but have not been provided as of the date of this report.

[148] In one decision the administrative judges questioned the quality of the investigative work undertaken by FEMA by including the following opinion of FEMA's substantiation of the denial for the replacement of Charity Hospital in New Orleans. "The FEMA representatives who testified at the hearing were less experienced and less credible than the BKA and RSMeans representatives. They had spent far less time in the building than had the BKA witnesses. Unlike the BKA and RSMeans witnesses, most of them were unlicensed. To the extent that FEMA relied on information in making the estimates on which version 3 of Project Worksheet 2175 was based, at least some of that information was incomplete; FEMA witnesses acknowledged that their estimates were subject to increase if FP&C presented appropriate proof that the facility's dimensions and disaster-related damages were greater than assumed by FEMA." CBCA 1741-FEMA, *In the Matter of State of Louisiana, Facility Planning and Control*, found at http://www.cbca.gsa.gov/2009FEMA/ DANIELS_01-27-10_1741-FEMA__STATE_OF_LOUISIANA,_FACILITY_PLAN NING_AND_CONTROL.pdf.

[149] Summary information on the requirements imposed on public assistance applicants is found at http://www.fema.gov/government/grant/pa/9580_5.shtm.

[150] 42 U.S.C. 5189a(c). The House committee report that accompanied the legislation containing this provision noted "The Committee intends that the President explore all available options to obtain a fair determination, including the consideration of alternative dispute resolution mechanisms to the extent they may be appropriate. The Committee intends to carefully oversee the implementation of this section." U.S. Congress, House, Committee on Public Works and Transportation, *Disaster Relief and Great Lakes Erosion Assistance*, 100th Cong., 2nd sess., H. Rpt. 100-517, March 15, 1988, p. 11. According to FEMA documentation available from the author of this report, the appeals provision derived from a proposal authored by then-Representative Tom Ridge; FEMA reportedly opposed the

inclusion of the provision in the statute. Unpublished document by Arthur Bennett of FEMA, *Legislative History of P.L. 100-707 and Proposed Amendments to Disaster Relief Act of 1974, 1980-1987*, pp. 90-91.

[151] Ernest Abbott, President, FEMA Law Associates, PLLC, *FLASH Newsletter*, vol. 4, ssue 12, September 2009, p. 2.

In: The Catastrophic Declaration Proposal...   ISBN: 978-1-61942-264-3
Editors: Landon West and Adrian Porter © 2012 Nova Science Publishers, Inc

Chapter 3

FEMA's Disaster Declaration Process: A Primer[*]

Francis X. McCarthy

SUMMARY

The Robert T. Stafford Disaster Relief and Emergency Assistance Act (referred to as the Stafford Act - 42 U.S.C. 5721 et seq.) authorizes the President to issue "major disaster" or "emergency" declarations before or after catastrophes occur. Emergency declarations trigger aid that protects property, public health, and safety and lessens or averts the threat of an incident becoming a catastrophic event. A major disaster declaration, issued after catastrophes occur, constitutes broader authority for federal agencies to provide supplemental assistance to help state and local governments, families and individuals, and certain nonprofit organizations recover from the incident.

The end result of a presidential disaster declaration is well known, if not entirely understood. Various forms of assistance are provided, including aid to families and individuals for uninsured needs and assistance to state and local governments and certain non-profits in rebuilding or replacing damaged infrastructure.

The amount of assistance provided through presidential disaster declarations has exceeded $140 billion. Often, in recent years, Congress has enacted supplemental appropriations legislation to cover

---

[*] This is an edited, reformatted and augmented version of a Congressional Research Service publication, CRS Report for Congress RL34146, from www.crs.gov, dated May 18, 2011.

unanticipated costs. While the amounts spent by the federal government on different programs may be reported, and the progress of the recovery can be observed, much less is known about the process that initiates all of this activity. Yet, it is a process that has resulted in an average of more than one disaster declaration a week over the last decade.

The disaster declaration procedure is foremost a process that preserves the discretion of the governor to request assistance and the President to decide to grant, or not to grant, supplemental help. The process employs some measurable criteria in two broad areas: Individual Assistance that aids families and individuals and Public Assistance that is mainly for repairs to infrastructure. The criteria, however, also considers many other factors, in each category of assistance, that help decision makers assess the impact of an event on communities and states.

Under current law, the decision to issue a declaration rests solely with the President. Congress has no formal role, but has taken actions to adjust the terms of the process. For example, P.L. 109-295 established an advocate to help small states with the declaration process. More recently, Congress introduced legislation, H.R. 3377, that would direct FEMA to update some of its criteria for considering Individual Assistance declarations.

Congress continues to examine the process and has received some recommendations for improvements. Given the importance of the decision, and the size of the overall spending involved, hearings have been held to review the declaration process so as to ensure fairness and equity in the process and its results.

BACKGROUND

Under the Robert T. Stafford Disaster Relief and Emergency Assistance Act (P.L. 93-288) there are two principal forms of presidential action to authorize federal supplemental assistance. Emergency declarations are made to protect property and public health and safety and to lessen or avert the threat of a major disaster or catastrophe.[1] Emergency declarations are often made when a threat is recognized (such as the emergency declarations for Hurricane Katrina which were made prior to landfall) and are intended to supplement and coordinate local and state efforts prior to the event such as evacuations and protection of public assets. In contrast, a major disaster declaration is made as a result of the disaster or catastrophic event and constitutes a broader authority that helps states and local communities, as well as families and individuals, recover from the damage caused by the event.[2] The differences between the two forms of declarations remain an area of study regarding what events may or may not qualify for the respective declarations.[3]

Federal disaster assistance has served as the impetus for many supplemental appropriations bills over the last several decades, and has accounted for presidential declarations in every state and territory.[4] The supplemental funds are placed in the Disaster Relief Fund (DRF) which is a "no-year" fund managed by the Federal Emergency Management Agency (FEMA) and used only for spending related to presidentially declared disasters.

Major disasters can be a dominant story in the mass media that captures attention both for the devastation that results as well as the potential help that is expected. As one observer noted:

> Disaster assistance is an almost perfect political currency. It serves humanitarian purposes that only the cynical academic could question. It is largely funded out of supplemental appropriations and thus does not officially add to the budget deficit. It promotes the local economy of the area where the building process occurs.[5]

While disaster assistance may be good "political currency," a disaster declaration is generally the result of a tragic and devastating incident that disrupts (and sometimes takes) the lives of hundreds or thousands of families and individuals and the communities and states where they reside. The long-term economic and environmental impact of a disaster can be severe. The assistance offered from federal and private sources may or may not be commensurate with the damage inflicted by a natural or man-made event. Following a disaster, years of rebuilding and recovery work may lie ahead for communities and states. It is the declaration process that sets the federal recovery help in motion.

The trigger for federal disaster assistance is contained in a relatively short statutory provision. P.L. 93-288 (the Stafford Act) includes one brief section that establishes the legal requirements for a major disaster declaration:

> Section 401. Procedures for Declaration. All requests for a declaration by the President that a major disaster exists shall be made by the Governor of the affected state. Such a request shall be based on a finding that the disaster is of such severity and magnitude that effective response is beyond the capabilities of the state and the affected local governments and that the federal assistance is necessary. As a part of such request, and as a prerequisite to major disaster assistance under this Act, the Governor shall take

appropriate response action under state law and direct execution of the state's emergency plan. The Governor shall furnish information on the nature and amount of State and local resources which have been or will be committed to alleviating the results of the disaster and shall certify that, for the current disaster, state and local government obligations and expenditures (of which state commitments must be a significant proportion) will comply with all applicable cost-sharing requirements of this Act. Based on the request of a Governor under this section, the President may declare under this Act that a major disaster or emergency exists.[6]

The process for an emergency declaration is also contained in the Stafford Act. In part it is similar to a major disaster declaration in finding and process, but the actual authorities are limited. In addition, section (b) provides for a special authority for the President to exercise his discretion for events that have a distinctly federal character:

> Sec. 5191. Procedure for declaration. (a) Request and declaration All requests for a declaration by the President that an emergency exists shall be made by the Governor of the affected State. Such a request shall be based on a finding that the situation is of such severity and magnitude that effective response is beyond the capabilities of the State and the affected local governments and that Federal assistance is necessary. As a part of such request, and as a prerequisite to emergency assistance under this chapter, the Governor shall take appropriate action under State law and direct execution of the State's emergency plan. The Governor shall furnish information describing the State and local efforts and resources which have been or will be used to alleviate the emergency, and will define the type and extent of Federal aid required. Based upon such Governor's request, the President may declare that an emergency exists. (b) Certain emergencies involving Federal primary responsibility. The President may exercise any authority vested in him by section 5192 of this title or section 5193 of this title with respect to an emergency when he determines that an emergency exists for which the primary responsibility for response rests with the United States because the emergency involves a subject area for which, under the Constitution or laws of the United States, the United States and authority. In determining whether or not such an emergency exists, the President shall consult the Governor of any affected State, if practicable. The President's determination may be made without regard to subsection (a) of this section.[7]

The declaration process is elaborated upon in regulations, specifically in Subpart B of Part 206 (44 CFR). While these regulations have been adjusted through the regulatory process during the past three decades, since 1974 the procedures have undergone little significant change. The process itself is representative of the historical progression of federal disaster relief from being of an episodic nature to the current commonplace disaster declaration, now occurring on a weekly basis. The context in which disaster relief has grown has been in keeping with the growth of government and its concerns.

> Federal disaster relief has a long history in the U.S. dating back to the last years of the eighteenth century and arguably provided much of the political genesis for the New Deal social welfare programs (Landis 1999; Landis 1998; Moss 1999). As Michele Landis argues, social and political construction of claimants for relief as helpless victims of external forces beyond their control ("Acts of God") have exerted an enduring influence on American political discourse, which has manifested itself in heavy reliance on prior political precedents and analogies in constructing responses to current disasters.[8]

Information contained in the Preliminary Damage Assessments (PDAs) and summaries prepared by FEMA regional offices that accompany gubernatorial requests were long considered "pre-decisional and deliberative information" by the executive branch because they are part of the package that is developed and sent to the White House for the President's review and ultimate decision. These materials have generally not been available under the Freedom of Information Act process.[9] However, during 2008, FEMA began to list on its website the results of the PDAs. While the summaries of FEMA recommendations are still not available, the agreed upon figures from the PDAs are now available to the public for review.[10]

Policy makers have found it difficult to achieve equity in the treatment of disparate natural disaster events. The events can vary widely in their type, scope, duration, and impact. Perhaps the greatest variables are the states they affect. Each state has a different topography, a different history, and different capacities to respond and recover based on their own authorities, resources, and choices in what they will do following a disaster. Given those variations, it is a daunting task to construct a uniform process that can account for the range of natural and governmental circumstances that are a part of the nation's potential disaster landscape.

CONGRESS AND THE DECLARATION PROCESS

The Impetus for Reform

The question of how the federal disaster declaration process should work has come to the attention of Congress from time to time. Congress has requested reports from its investigative arms and investigated the process in panels that have considered aspects of the disaster relief process.[11] Various administrations have also considered the process and FEMA's role in it.

In 1981, and again in 2001, GAO issued reports on the declaration process that questioned the quality and consistency of FEMA's assessment criteria as well as the agency's ability to produce valid recommendations to the President on a governor's request for supplemental aid. As the most recent report (2001) concluded:

> These criteria are not necessarily indicative of a state's ability to pay for the damage because they do not consider the substantial differences in states' financial capacities to respond when disasters occur. As a result, federal funds may be provided for some disasters when they are not needed – a result that would be inconsistent with the Stafford Act's intent.[12]

Congressional interest in the declaration process derived, in part, from the increased cost in emergency spending—a recurring subject for the appropriations committees when considering supplemental spending legislation.[13] One review of disaster funding, particularly supplemental appropriations, found that the great majority of Disaster Relief Fund spending is related to the large, catastrophic events that meet the criteria established in the Stafford Act. These supplementals have been "driven" by the urgency of large natural disasters. As one witness explained in congressional testimony:

> Since funds provided in annual appropriations measures may be used to cover the federal costs of less catastrophic major disasters, Congress has focused critical attention on "must pass" legislation that would replenish the Disaster Relief Fund for the worst and most costly disasters.[14]

A review of data for a seven-year period from 1988 to 1995 reveals that large expenditures, as funded by supplemental bills, relate to declarations issued for the largest events.[15] During this time period, disaster declarations were made for Hurricane Hugo, the Loma Prieta earthquake, Hurricane

Andrew, the Midwest floods of 1993, and the Northridge earthquake. However, these were not the only events deemed worthy of presidential action and of cost to the federal treasury. As summarized by one author:

> But like the tail of a comet, over 200 other declarations accounted for one quarter of such outlays, many of them of relatively minute cost and extent. While of lesser impact on the national treasury, such "low end" declarations have become, to some observers, new sources of federal spending at the local level, long referred to in other contexts as "pork barrel spending."[16]

During early 2001, the term "entitlement" was beginning to be used in describing federal disaster spending by the new Bush Administration. Underlining this thinking in his first appearance before the Senate Appropriations Committee, FEMA Director Joe M. Allbaugh explained:

> FEMA is looking at ways to develop a meaningful and objective criteria for disaster declarations that can be applied consistently. These criteria will not preclude the President's discretion but will help states better understand when they can reasonably turn to the federal government for assistance and when it would be more appropriate for the state to handle the disaster itself.[17]

During the 110th Congress, attention was given to the disaster declaration process and what states and local governments can reasonably expect from that process. During the early spring of 2007, there were tornadoes that had an impact on Arkansas, Alabama and Georgia. The latter two states received disaster declarations while the damage in Arkansas was deemed insufficient to warrant federal assistance. Following these actions, Chairman Bennie Thompson of the House Homeland Security Committee scheduled a hearing to review FEMA's procedures. Representative Thompson set the context as follows:

> As Members representing real communities back home, we want to understand just how FEMA makes determinations regarding what is a disaster deserving of attention and when folks have to fend for themselves. Quite simply, we must have a serious discussion on what our expectations are of our federal government and what should remain a state and local responsibility.[18]

In order to examine the process and the financial projections of disaster spending in particular, Congress mandated in P.L. 110-28 that GAO study how FEMA develops its estimates for supplemental funding that may be needed.[19] Report language detailed these instructions for the review:

> The Committee continues to be concerned with FEMA's ability to manage resources in a manner that maximizes its ability to effectively and efficiently deal with disasters. One aspect of particular concern is how FEMA makes projections of funding needed in response to any given disaster or to meet future disasters. A recent Government Accountability Office (GAO) report raised concerns about FEMA's ability to manage its day-to-day resources and the lack of information on how FEMA's resources are aligned with its operations. As a follow-up to this report, the Committee requests that within six months of enactment GAO review how FEMA develops its estimates of the funds needed to respond to any given disaster. Such review should include how FEMA makes initial estimates, how FEMA refines those estimates within the first few months of a disaster, and how closely FEMA's estimates predict actual costs. The review should also include additional analysis and recommendations regarding FEMA's ability to manage disaster-related resources in a manner that maximizes effective execution of its mission.[20]

The study parameters mandated by Congress are broader than the declaration process, placing its emphasis on ongoing FEMA spending, including the refinement and revision of early estimates as well as the general management of spending projections for the Disaster Relief Fund (DRF). But it recognizes the importance of the initial estimates in decision-making and that the declaration process represents the fundamental decision to both establish federal participation following a disaster and provides the initial estimated amount of resources needed that informs that decision.

GAO's eventual report in response to this request suggested that FEMA's estimates for disaster costs have improved but could use additional refinement; for example

> some of the factors that can lead to changes in FEMA's cost estimates are beyond its control, such as the discovery of hidden damage. Others are not, such as its management of mission assignments. Sensitivity analyses to identify the marginal effect of key cost drivers could provide FEMA a way to isolate and mitigate the effect of these factors on its early estimates. To better predict applicant costs for the Individual Assistance program, FEMA could

substitute or add more geographically specific indicators for its national average[21]

During the 111th Congress, a hearing before the House Homeland Security Committee focusing on FEMA's regional offices also elicited comments regarding the relative speed, and perceived lack of transparency, of the declaration process. The comments came from both a committee member and a state official closely involved in the process.

> Ranking Republican Mike D. Rogers of Alabama questioned the timeliness of FEMA's disaster declarations. Declarations that should take a few days often take a month or longer, and a lack of available information on the status of requests only adds to state officials' frustration, said Brock Long, director of Alabama's Emergency Management Agency. "When we make phone calls to the region or to headquarters, a lot of time the answer we get is 'the declaration request is in process' and that's it," Long said. [22]

The Skepticism of Reform

There have been several proposals to impose more stringent regulations on the declaration process in an attempt to more precisely assess disaster impacts, calculate eligible damage, and incorporate some measure of suffering and loss. Differing perceptions of the declaration process resulted in different reactions to these proposed reforms.

The history of the disaster declaration process is rife with reform efforts that were perceived by some not as reform but as punitive measures directed at certain constituencies. Some of those differing perceptions were held by those closest to the event at the local level that had experienced a disaster. A different perception was also often held by governors that wanted to protect their option to request federal help. These perceptions were also shared, in some instances, by Members of Congress representing affected areas. All elected officials argued, in various forms, that reform should not impede the delivery of needed federal aid.

One example, now in law, of the desire to reform but not obstruct the declaration process is in the Post-Katrina Emergency Management Reform Act of October of 2006. That statute created a new position at FEMA: the Small State and Rural Advocate.[23] One of the principal duties of the advocate is to ensure that the needs of smaller states and rural communities will be "met in the declaration process;" the advocate is also directed to "help small states prepare declaration requests, among other duties."[24]

Another example was FEMA's response to recommendations from GAO's 1981 report. FEMA drafted regulations in 1986 that would be more certain in their delineation of state requirements prior to a declaration, reduce overall federal contributions, and install a formula to determine whether a state would receive a presidential disaster declaration for repairs to state and local infrastructure (known as "public assistance" in the Stafford Act). As the congressional report on the initiative summarized the FEMA draft:

> The proposal would have limited the number of future presidential declarations by establishing a "state deductible" based on a per capita minimum dollar amount adjusted by the ratio of the state/local price index to the national index. Of 111 declarations issued in prior years, 61 would have been ineligible for any public assistance. FEMA also proposed to decrease the federal share for disaster costs from 75 percent to 50 percent and to exclude aid to special districts.[25]

The FEMA proposal of 20 years ago addressed some problems identified by students and critics of the declaration process. However, some Members of Congress viewed this proposal as a means of removing the power of discretion from elected leadership. Rather than apply the empirical solution suggested by FEMA to perceived problems in the declaration process, Congress instead legislated a provision to explicitly forbid the primacy of any "arithmetic formula." In place of agreeing to the regulatory changes in the formula proposed by FEMA and the Administration, Congress added the following section to the Stafford Act:

> Limitation on the Use of Sliding Scales. Section 320. No geographic area shall be precluded from receiving assistance under this Act solely by virtue of an arithmetic formula or sliding scale based on income or population.[26]

While enactment of this legislation halted FEMA's efforts, the issue did not disappear. As discussed below, FEMA has since adopted regulations that use, but not "solely", arithmetic formulae in determining need for assistance.

PRESIDENTIAL AND GUBERNATORIAL DISCRETION

The declaration process contains many factors for consideration and, for all but the most catastrophic events, the process moves at a deliberate speed accumulating information from several sources. While the process is informed by that information and its relationship to potential assistance programs, the information that is gathered at the state and local level does not preclude the exercise of judgment by the governor or the President.

The Stafford Act stipulates several procedural actions a governor must take prior to requesting federal disaster assistance (including the execution within the state of the state emergency plan and an agreement to accept cost-share provisions and related information-sharing). Still, the process leaves broad discretion with the governor if he or she determines that a situation is "beyond the capabilities of the state." The concession that a state can no longer respond on its own is difficult to quantify. It is the governor who makes that assessment, based on his or her knowledge of state resources and capabilities.

Actions by a governor are a driving constant in this process. Both declarations of major disaster and declarations of emergency must be triggered by a request to the President from the governor of the affected state.[27] The President cannot issue either an emergency or a major disaster declaration without a gubernatorial request. The only exception to this rule is the authority given to the President to declare an emergency when "he determines that an emergency exists for which the primary responsibility for response rests with the United States because the emergency involves a subject area for which, under the Constitution or laws of the United States, the United States can exercise exclusive or preeminent responsibility and authority."[28]

The importance of governors in the process is not lost on, nor would it likely be diminished by, Presidents who formerly served in that position. Over the last three decades of Stafford Act implementation, four of the Presidents during this period were former governors who had worked through the disaster declaration process from both the state and the federal level.[29]

Having that experience may have left the Presidents, and their staffs and appointees, with an appreciation of the discretionary authority inherent in the process. While there are some established standards in the law, the factors that are to be weighed in considering the impact of a disaster on the need for assistance for families and individuals are general considerations that underscore the judgment required to reach a decision. As one observer noted of the decision for general, flexible considerations:

In other words, Congress likes to keep the process imprecise, even if
benefits occasionally go to the undeserving. The absence of objective criteria
preserves wide political discretion to the president.30

Congress also has among its number former governors who have
exercised this discretion at the state level. Still, despite the interest some may
have in keeping "the process imprecise," some Members of Congress express
disappointment at times with the exercise of the discretion and the general
nature of the considerations. As noted previously in this report, that
disappointment has been reflected in hearings that have focused on how the
disaster declaration process works in practice.

In the declaration process, FEMA develops a recommendation that is sent
to the White House for action. However, as implied, it is a recommendation
from FEMA and the Department of Homeland Security (DHS). The final
action, as defined in the regulations of the process, is a "Presidential
determination."[31] Just as the governor retains the discretion to request
federal assistance regardless of thresholds or indicators, the President retains
the discretion to make a decision that may be counter to recommendations
he receives.

PRELIMINARY DAMAGE ASSESSMENTS

Although not explicitly mentioned in the Stafford Act, Preliminary
Damage Assessments (PDAs) are a crucial part of the process of determining
if an event may be declared a major disaster by the President. The minimal
discussion of PDAs in the public record stands in inverse proportion to their
impact on disaster decisions and subsequent expenditures from the Disaster
Relief Fund (DRF).

When a PDA is conducted after an event it is the "mechanism used to
determine the impact and magnitude of damage and the resulting unmet needs
of individuals, businesses, the public sector, and the community as a whole."[32]
The most "preliminary" part of a PDA may be an abbreviated one completed
only by the state to determine if the situation merits development of a
complete PDA with federal participation. Based on their previous experience,
states may determine that the event will not reach the level where a federal
disaster declaration is likely. However, despite findings that federal aid may
not be needed, there may be political considerations that could lead to a
gubernatorial request. As one author points out in his study of the process:

Governors also feel the heat of media coverage of incidents in their states, and they too appreciate the importance of exhibiting political responsiveness. Governors also appreciate that their future political fortunes may be influenced by how they handle their disaster and emergency incidents. As a consequence, the hypothesis assumes that governors are the pivotal and decisive players in securing presidential disaster declarations and that they have a tendency to request declarations for even marginal events[33]

While media and political pressure may have some influence on the outcome of some requests, governors may exercise caution since they are reluctant to be turned down when requesting aid. A denial of their request could be perceived by some to reflect adversely on their decision-making skills and judgment under pressure. Unlike the procedures of the federal process, a governor's decision to request a declaration is a public and often newsworthy action.

Regardless of any question regarding motivation, the governor's first decision is whether the incident is severe enough to assemble a traditional PDA team to survey the damaged area. The traditional PDA team includes a state official, representatives from the appropriate FEMA regional office, a local official familiar with the area and, in some instances, representatives from the American Red Cross and/or the Small Business Administration. The FEMA representatives have the responsibility of briefing the team on the factors to be considered, the information that will be helpful in the assessment and how the information should be reported. One significant improvement in this process is that the regulations now require that the participants reconcile any differences in their findings.[34]

Another factor is the quality of the PDA team and its findings. PDAs are ordered up quickly after an event. FEMA's 10 regional offices are often engaged in multiple disasters and have to rely on temporary employees (albeit, usually experienced ones) to staff the PDA team.[35] Also, given the variables among regions in interpreting policy and guidance, consistency of approach may also be a question. This became a significant issue during the hurricane season of 2004 in Florida, where questions were raised regarding the designations of some counties.[36]

When working openly and with federal and state cooperation, the PDA can be an effective and inclusive process. As Washington State Emergency Management Director Jim Mullen, and FEMA Region X Director Susan Reinertson, explained the process for a survey of flood damage in November of 2006:

'Joint PDA teams will visit and inspect damaged areas, document damage and talk, as needed, with homeowners and local officials,' said Mullen. 'It's a partnership effort designed to provide a clear picture of the extent and locations of damage in counties that have reported the most substantial damage to primary homes and businesses.'

'The PDA teams look at the total scope of damage to establish if recovery is beyond the capabilities and resources of the state and local governments. The PDA doesn't determine the total cost of recovery, nor does it guarantee a presidential declaration for individual assistance,' said FEMA Regional Director Susan Reinertson.[37]

PDA teams often face challenges in the collection of data. Some information may be observable in a survey of the area, such as the number of bridges damaged or the number of culverts washed out. But other necessary information, such as the percentage of elderly residents in an area, or the amount of insurance coverage for all homeowners or renters may be more difficult to obtain. Also the geographic span of the damage can create complications as the PDA team struggles to cover all of the affected area in a limited time. Further complications may then ensue based on how much of the area that the PDA teams have visited (generally counties) are included in the governor's request.

While PDAs are the usual way damages are assessed, there are exceptions to this rule. Some incidents are so massive in their scale and impact that the actual declaration is not in doubt. This would include events such as Hurricanes Andrew and Katrina, the Loma Prieta and Northridge earthquakes, the Mount St. Helens volcanic eruption, and the September 11 terrorist attacks. In these instances, the decision is not whether a declaration will be made, but how broad the coverage will be, both geographic and programmatic. In such cases the President, in accordance with the regulations, can waive the PDA requirement. But as the regulations note, a PDA may still be needed "to determine unmet needs for managerial response purposes."[38] This means the PDA helps to identify a specific, potential need for certain programs, such as crisis counseling or disaster unemployment assistance during the disaster recovery period. It is this identification of discrete need that helps the governor decide on which assistance programs will be requested.

The PDA is a "bottom up" process as information gradually rises up for decision-makers to consider. Multiple pressure points, including affected citizens, elected officials, and professionals in various fields, may all urge PDA team members to reach certain conclusions. As one author suggests:

The president, motivated by the need to appear highly politically responsive, solicits and encourages a gubernatorial request for a presidential disaster declaration. Publicity is a factor in that CNN and other news organizations help to promote nationally what would otherwise be a local incident addressed by subnational authorities. The president may also be influenced by the electoral importance of the state that experiences the incident.[39]

It is difficult to overstate the importance of the media context as noted above. Depending on the news of the day, the disaster event in question may be the biggest national story and thus create momentum for action that is difficult to assuage with explanations of traditional administrative procedures.

FACTORS CONSIDERED FOR PUBLIC ASSISTANCE IN MAJOR DISASTER DECLARATIONS

Public Assistance (PA) refers to various categories of assistance to state and local governments and non-profit organizations. Principally, PA covers the repairs or replacement of infrastructure (roads, bridges, public buildings, etc.) but also includes debris removal and emergency protective measures which cover additional costs for local public safety groups incurred by their actions in responding to the disaster.[40] In assessing the degree of PA damage, FEMA considers six general areas:

- Estimated cost of the assistance
- Localized impacts
- Insurance coverage
- Hazard mitigation
- Recent multiple disasters
- Programs of other federal assistance.

Estimated Cost of the Assistance

Although all of these factors are considered, the *estimated cost of the assistance* is a key component and may be "more equal" than other factors since it contains a threshold figure. What is especially noteworthy about the cost estimates is that they could be interpreted as an example of the "arithmetic formula" that was precluded from use in Section 320 of the Stafford Act. However, that section does state that a formula cannot be "solely" determinative of the fate of a governor's request. Use of the other factors listed arguably justifies FEMA's consideration of the threshold figure of $1 million in PA damage—the first number FEMA expects to see in a request that includes PA as an area of needed assistance. In addition FEMA also considers a state-wide threshold of $1.30 per capita in estimated eligible disaster costs before it will approve a request for PA help.[41]

Depending on the state's population, the per capita threshold may be difficult to reach. For example, the 2000 Census estimated California's population at just under 34 million people.[42] Applying the $1.30 per capita figure, it would require eligible PA damage in California to be close to $41.5 million. California is a large state with a budget and tax base commensurate with its size. Expecting a large state to be able to respond on its own is equating such help, and such amounts, to be within "the capabilities of the state."[43]

Compare that level of eligible damage for California ($41.5 million) with Nevada, a small population state according to FEMA regulations.[44] For Nevada, with a population of just under 2 million people according to the 2000 Census, eligible PA damage of about $2.4 million would make the state potentially eligible for supplemental federal assistance.

There are obvious differences in the populations of these two states; however, both have substantial industries and are growing areas. They are bordering states that are both subject to the threat of earthquake damage.[45] Different measurements have been suggested to try to more accurately capture a state's capacity to respond to disaster events. Some of these measurements are discussed in the "Congressional Considerations for the Declaration Process" section of this report.

Localized Impacts

The next factor used by FEMA to consider a declaration that may include PA help focuses on *localized impacts*. FEMA generally looks for a minimum of $3.27 per capita in infrastructure damage in a county before designating it for PA funding.[46] While such a per capita amount would likely ensure that the local entity (almost always a county) would be included in the list of jurisdictions designated for PA assistance should a declaration be issued, high local levels of damage per capita would not supersede a finding that damages state-wide fell below the statewide threshold amount. However, knowledge of a very large localized impact could weigh on the President's discretion and raise the importance of the *localized impact* factor.

Insurance Coverage

Insurance coverage also is considered in assessing damage. Officials preparing PA estimates deduct the amount of insurance that should have been held by units of governments and nonprofit organizations from the total eligible damage amount. However, this is a complicated assessment with several caveats. A considerable number of states and local governments "self-insure" their investments against some types of disasters and may argue that they would have total liability absent a federal disaster declaration.[47] Also, in the event of some disasters (earthquakes being a prime example), the state insurance commissioner must certify that hazard insurance is both available and affordable. If it is not available, deducting an amount of coverage not realistically available would not be a practical consideration.[48]

In the case of a flood event, it is much simpler for FEMA to access information available on whether flood insurance was available, given that FEMA administers the National Flood Insurance Program (NFIP) and there are program staff in each FEMA region who monitor NFIP participation. This knowledge of flood insurance availability and costs makes it a simpler process for FEMA to deduct the amount of flood insurance that should have been in place from the total potential award for a public structure.[49]

Hazard Mitigation

Hazard mitigation presents a challenging and different type of consideration for Public Assistance disaster declaration requests. If the requesting state can prove that their per capita amount of infrastructure damage falls short due to mitigation measures that lessened the disaster's impact, FEMA will consider that favorably in its recommendation to the President. Calculations of savings would be dependant on cost-benefit analysis and other related estimates of damages that were avoided. This factor is intended to encourage mitigation projects by states to lessen the risks of future natural disasters. Some might consider this practice to be one where "a good deed should go unpunished." However, another factor to be considered is that the mitigation work that is credited to the state may, in fact, have been principally financed (up to 75% of the costs) with previous FEMA disaster assistance funding through the Hazard Mitigation Grant Program (HMGP).[50]

Recent Multiple Disasters

Recent multiple disasters is the factor FEMA considers when a state has been repeatedly hit by disaster events (either presidential declarations or events within the state that were not declared) within the previous 12 months. FEMA evaluates the amount of funds that the state has committed to these recent events and their impact on the state and its residents. For example, a request from a state that has responded on it own to a series of tornadoes may receive a more favorable consideration, even if the catalyst for the request was arguably not as destructive as others. This factor was used recently in FEMA's assessment of the multiple hurricanes that struck Florida during the 2004 hurricane season.

Other Federal Programs

When FEMA is reviewing a governor's request it is also considering whether *other federal programs* are available. One example might be if a large amount of the reported damage occurred to federal-aid-system roads. The Federal Highway Administration (FHWA) is a more appropriate agency to handle such an event, and administers programs that address this specific type of damage.[51] The bridge collapse in Minnesota in August of 2007 was a dramatic example of this type of event that would warrant significant, non-FEMA, federal aid. Similarly, other federal programs may be more responsive to certain types of natural events and the problems they create. For example, oceanic bacteria could cause harmful failures for the fishing and hatcheries industry. Should such outbreaks occur, the Magnuson-Stevens Fisheries Act (P.L. 94-265) authorizes programs under the Commerce Department that would have more appropriate forms of emergency assistance for commercial fishermen than FEMA through the Stafford Act.[52] Also, while drought is a type of disaster that could result in a major disaster, such catastrophes usually result in program assistance from the U.S. Department of Agriculture rather than presidential declarations.[53]

In summary, all of these factors are used by FEMA to determine whether a major disaster declaration will be recommended and whether PA aid will be extended as a part of that potential declaration. FEMA's assistance to a homeowner who chooses not to purchase insurance is left with help from FEMA that is capped at $28,200. The assistance to repair public infrastructure is based on the amount of eligible damage caused by the disaster event. There is no cap, and the sums can be in the billions of dollars.

FACTORS CONSIDERED FOR INDIVIDUAL ASSISTANCE IN MAJOR DISASTER DECLARATIONS

Individual Assistance (IA) includes various forms of help for families and individuals following a disaster event. The assistance authorized by the Stafford Act can include housing assistance, disaster unemployment assistance, crisis counseling and other programs intended to address the needs of people. In seeking to assess the impact of a disaster on families and individuals, the factors FEMA considers include:

- Concentration of damages
- Trauma
- Special populations
- Voluntary agency assistance
- Insurance coverage
- Average amount of Individual Assistance by state.

Concentration of Damages

Concentration of damages looks at the density of the damage in individual communities. FEMA's regulations state that highly concentrated damages "generally indicate a greater need for federal assistance than widespread and scattered damages throughout a state."[54] Concentrated damages are far more visible and may be an indication of significant damage to infrastructure supporting neighborhoods and communities, thereby increasing the needs of individuals and families.

However, the dispersion of damage is not necessarily an indication that individual and family needs are non-existent. Damage in rural states, almost by definition, is far less concentrated and could arguably be more difficult for a PDA team to view and assess. Congress has sought to address this challenge through the creation of the Rural and Small State advocate position at FEMA.[55]

Trauma

Trauma is defined in three ways in FEMA's regulations: the loss of life and injuries, the disruption of normal community functions, and emergency needs that could include an extended loss of power or water.[56]

Despite their prominence and importance to victims, families and communities, the loss of life and injuries have relatively little bearing on a declaration decision, but they would greatly influence media coverage that can influence the decision-making process.

An extreme amount of losses would be traumatic and considered in the evaluation of the governor's request. But the actual help available from FEMA in response to such losses is limited. The Other Needs Assistance (ONA) program, a part of the Individuals and Households Program (IHP), may provide assistance for uninsured funeral expenses and medical help.[57]

As noted, the extreme loss of life or many injuries will likely influence the amount of media coverage for the event. As previously explained in the "Presidential and Gubernatorial Discretion" section of this report, the media coverage can influence not merely the pace of the decision, but the actual decision itself.[58]

The other areas (disruption of functions and loss of utilities) in the trauma rubric can be a point of dispute in declaration decisions. What constitutes a disruption of normal community functions?

Do road closures that result in the closing of schools equate to a disruption? Another consideration is how long the disruption remains and how, or even if, federal help can alleviate the disruption. Similarly, the emergency needs due to the loss of utilities are defined by the length of time the power or water are not in service. Because characteristics of these factors are not defined in regulations, discretionary judgments are significant aspects of the evaluation of IA needs.

Special populations are considered by FEMA in assessing a request for Individual Assistance.

Special Populations

FEMA attempts to ascertain information about the demographics of an area affected by a disaster event. Those demographics include the age and income of residents, the amount of home ownership in an area, the effect on Native American tribal groups, and other related considerations to be taken into account. The knowledge of the demographics within the affected area gives FEMA added information to consider regarding trauma and community disruption. Special populations are a factor in the consideration of a governor's request, but the total number of households affected that would be eligible for Stafford Act programs remains the prime consideration.

Voluntary Agency Assistance

Voluntary agency assistance involves an evaluation of what the volunteer and charitable groups and state and local governments have already done to assist disaster victims as well as the potential help they can offer in the recovery period. FEMA also considers whether state or local programs "can meet the needs of disaster victims."[59] This factor is among the most contentious in the disaster declaration process due to the subjectivity of the assessment.

FEMA's evaluation of local and state capabilities, and the capabilities of the local voluntary community, may vary greatly among catastrophes. There is an expectation that the regional office's relationship and history with the state could provide some of this information. But a cursory look at state programs available to "meet the needs of disaster victims" suggests that few resources are comparable to federal help in intent or in scope. A National Emergency Management Association (NEMA) survey of its members for state-funded disaster assistance showed that relatively few states provide assistance beyond that authorized in the Stafford Act.

NEMA noted that the "other" category could include a range of programs or funds not necessarily of direct aid to victims, including "local government loans, HAZMAT (hazardous materials) funds, disaster unemployment insurance, and a governor's contingency fund."[60] The report does not define these programs any further, but the small numbers of programs directed at IA or unmet needs suggests that FEMA officials evaluate this area carefully given the lack of information regarding available resources for these programs and the extent of their coverage.[61]

Table 1 summarizes data from that survey

Assistance Provided	Number of States with These Programs
Public Assistance Program	22
Individual Assistance Program	9
Unmet Need Program	1
Other	5

Source: NEMA 2010 Biennial Report: Organizations & Funding for State Emergency
   Management and Homeland Security (Lexington, KY: Council of State
   Governments) p. 4.

In the same vein, attempts to assess the capacity of local voluntary and charitable groups to handle "unmet needs" caused by a disaster can be challenging and problematic. Part of the challenge is discerning the assistance available from the non-profit, voluntary sector, and if that aid meets the needs created by the disaster event. A problematic aspect of the assessment is similar to the "good deeds" concept addressed in the "hazard mitigation" factor in PA. In that instance, the criteria reward the mitigation work that communities and states had undertaken to lessen the impact of a disaster. Similarly, a strong and efficient charitable sector at the local level that is equipped and funded to address the remaining needs could result in a disaster not being declared and federal supplemental funding not being made available.

Arguably, a community does not base all of its preparedness decisions on the potential of FEMA funding in an extraordinary situation. However, it has been argued that some aspects of the FEMA declaration process could be viewed as disincentives for a sound, local capacity to deliver such assistance. One analyst believed that this problem underlines the need for clear criteria for smaller disaster events:

> Too low a threshold reinforces the perception that the federal government will always come like the cavalry to rescue states and local governments from their improvident failure to prepare for routine disasters. Lapses in preparedness, response, recovery, and mitigation (to cite the disaster management litany) should not be encouraged by a too readily available bailout by the federal government and taxpayers.62

In evaluating the capabilities of local organizations, FEMA seeks to determine the help that actually exists, rather than assistance that might be expected to be in place.

Insurance Coverage

As noted earlier in the PA section, *insurance coverage* is also an important consideration when FEMA considers a request for Individual Assistance. This is in part derived from the general prohibition in the statute of the duplication of benefits, as follows:

> ... each federal agency administering any program providing financial assistance to persons, business concerns, or other entities suffering losses as a result of a major disaster or emergency, shall assure that no such person, business concern or other entity will receive such assistance with respect to any part of such loss as to which he has received financial assistance under any other program or from insurance or any other source.[63]

This provision does not necessarily result in delayed assistance. FEMA is able to provide help to individuals and households that have disaster damages but are waiting on insurance or other assistance for help. Those applicants can receive FEMA help as long as they agree to reimburse FEMA when they receive their other assistance. If a disaster occurred where almost all of the damaged dwellings were fully insured for the damage that was sustained, FEMA could conclude that a disaster declaration by the President was not necessary. Among the types of disasters FEMA frequently responds to, tornado disasters particularly reflect this challenge since tornado coverage is a part of most homeowners insurance policies.

Since the NFIP is administered by FEMA, officials can quickly determine the status of flood insurance in communities and the number of policies in place in the affected area. Additionally, knowledge of the income of the area's residents, as suggested in the *special populations* factor, allows the agency to make some projections regarding the likelihood of insurance coverage, particularly special hazard insurance such as flood or earthquake insurance, which are potentially expensive additions to a homeowners policy. As one analyst has noted:

> The decision not to buy insurance for earthquakes, floods, hurricanes and other natural disasters isn't always conscious: some homeowners don't realize they're not already covered. But many others, faced with high premiums and policies with limited coverage, gamble that they won't need insurance help to rebuild after a disaster.64

Average Amount of Individual Assistance by State

The last factor FEMA considers in assessing IA needs is the *average amount of Individual Assistance by state.* FEMA has issued statistics on average losses but notes that the average numbers used are not a threshold (see *Table 2*). The agency does suggest that the "following averages may prove useful to states and voluntary agencies as they develop plans and programs to meet the needs of disaster victims." The inference is that the levels listed generally are what would be expected in damage to dwellings.

Table 2. Average Amount of Federal Assistance Per Disaster Based on Size of State, July 1995 - July 1999

Categories	Small States <2MillionPopulation	Medium States 2-10 Million Population	Large States >10 Million Population
Avg. population (1990 Census Data)	1,000,057	4,713,548	15,552,791
Number of disaster housing applications approved	1,507	2,747	4,679
Number of homes est. major damage/destroyed	173	582	801
Dollar amount of housing assistance	$2.8 million	$4.6 million	$9.5 million
Number of Individual and Family Grants (IFG) approved (Now known as ONA)	495	1,377	2,071
Dollar amount of IFG assistance (now ONA)	$1.1 million	$2.9 million	$4.6 million
Disaster housing/IFG (ONA) combined assistance	$3.9 million	$7.5 million	$ 14.1 million

Source: 44 CFR §206.48(b) (6).

The average numbers that follow are based on disasters that occurred between July of 1995 and July of 1999; the data are 10 years old and of questionable use today. The chart divides states into three categories: small states (under 2 million in population), medium states (2 to 10 million in population) and large states (over 10 million in population). The population amounts are based on the 1990 Census.

While FEMA's regulations stress that these are not thresholds, they are considered by agency officials in determining whether IA will be provided. Presumably states may consider that FEMA help could be forthcoming if damage reaches the state indicator levels. However, since the amounts have not been updated in ten years and are based on a 1990 census, it is difficult to determine the degree to which these numbers are considered. Given Congress's mandate in Section 320 of the Stafford Act, this cannot be an arithmetic formula that solely determines whether assistance is provided. But the presentation of loss indicators may guide states when considering whether to request assistance.

In addition to the issue of the data's currency, a larger and more compelling question is whether the numbers in the chart match up to the Preliminary Damage Assessments (PDAs) for those events. Absent an existing review of detailed information in PDA forms, it is not possible to determine the usefulness of the data in *Table 2*.[65] Still, given the level of experience in this field following literally thousands of disaster declarations over the last 30 years, it could be argued that the numbers of eligible households assisted may be reflective of the estimated damage upon which the decision for a disaster declaration was made.

Congressional Considerations for the Declaration Process

When Congress considers the mandated GAO reports and other commentary on the declaration process, there are some considerations that Members may wish to review when considering the current declaration process.

The Composition of Preliminary Damage Assessment Teams

One area of consideration is the composition of Preliminary Damage Assessment teams. Team members are involved throughout the process and include local officials guiding the team, state personnel who assist the governor in requesting assistance, and FEMA staff who work on the disaster if one is declared. While FEMA staff have the opportunity at several levels to refine the information the team gathers on damages and to ask additional questions, the process could be approached in other ways. Some FEMA staff have suggested the formation of several permanent teams that would have PDAs as their prime job task without continuing involvement in particular disasters. This could result in more consistent assessments with the bonus of added perspective of team members with exposure to various disasters in many regions of the country. Establishing independent and expert on-site groups to review a situation is a recommendation that the National Transportation Safety Board (NTSB) has been contemplating in their investigations of transportation accidents.[66]

The PDA is an important part of the declaration process. While it can be subject to challenge, it is also the assessment closest to the event. Given its vital role in the process the PDA deserves close attention to determine if these on-site assessments are accurately reflecting the character of an event and the likely eligible damages following a disaster event.

Updating and Revising Individual Assistance Averages

As previously noted, the averages that appear in FEMA's declaration process regulations for Individual Assistance (IA) to states are derived from experiences from July 1995 to July 1999.[67] These figures could be updated based on FEMA's more recent experience in delivering this type of assistance. Legislation introduced in the 111th Congress had a provision that directed FEMA to review the factors that are considered for an IA designation.[68]

While the averages are separated by state population size, there does not appear to be a threshold number equivalent to the PA figure of $1 million in eligible damage. In the case of IA help, a dollar figure may not be desirable; however, numbers of families and households affected, or a minimum number of homes with major damage, could potentially be a starting point in establishing a base IA threshold for consideration of requests.

Other Potential Disaster Indicators

The current per capita indicator based on state population according to the U.S. Census is clear, but some observers believe it lacks precision. For example, the earlier discussion on PA indicators pointed out the commonality between California and Nevada regarding earthquake risk as well as the growth of the states. Their population sizes are very different but the per capita indicator alone does not necessarily measure a state's fiscal capacity.

The GAO report in 2001 noted that per capita personal income measures do not take into account the taxable income a state may enjoy from businesses or corporations that may have considerable taxable profits. GAO did suggest a different indicator:

> We have previously reported that Total Taxable Resources (TTR), a measure developed by the U.S. Department of Treasury, is a better measure of state funding capacity in that it provides a more comprehensive measure of the resources that are potentially subject to state taxation.[69]

FEMA's response to this suggestion questioned whether the use of TTR would be in violation of the legislative prohibition against arithmetic formulas.[70] The TTR does have very specific information and also tracks growth within a state. However, this appears to make it a more accurate measurement. The degree of detail in the measurement would not necessarily make it the "sole" determinant of disaster aid. It could remain an indicator and one among several factors to be considered in the declaration process.

CONCLUDING OBSERVATIONS

The disaster declaration process, though subject to inquiry, argument, hearings, studies and recommendations, has changed very little over time. It remains a process that can be observed and evaluated as it occurs in the area affected by the disaster, and grows opaque as it moves up through layers of FEMA and DHS management to the White House. By making PDA information available, FEMA has begun to lift the veil on the decisions that are made. Congress has demonstrated an interest in this process and has sought to understand its limits and its effectiveness. "From the Government Accountability Office in 1981 to Vice President Gore's National Performance Review in 1994," one student of the process noted, "countless policy critiques have called for more objective criteria for presidential disaster declarations."[71] But those calls can be muted when a disaster occurs in a particular place that has particular importance to actors in the process, whether in Congress or the executive branch.

While criteria have been established to create a relatively uniform and knowable process, these criteria may not be determinative of the most critical elements considered. An emphasis on victims of unexpected natural disaster events will likely always have a compelling influence on the disaster declaration process. But since disaster relief does have a political element, at many levels, precedent arguably can have value in improving the declaration process so that it can be applied broadly and fairly. But precedent can also be problematic when discussing events of very different size and impact.

During the last Congress, attention was directed to the nature of the disaster declaration process. The 112th Congress may choose to consider a broad review of the process that might include the consistency of FEMA's approach across the nation in making damage assessments, other potential indicators of state capabilities and capacities, and the currency of the factors it employs to evaluate those assessments of disaster damage and the state requests on which they are based.

End Notes

[1] 42 U.S.C. § 5122.

[2] Ibid.

[3] For additional discussion, see CRS Report RL34724, *Would an Influenza Pandemic Qualify as a Major Disaster Under the Stafford Act?*, by Edward C. Liu.

[4] For more information on disaster supplementals, see CRS Report RL33226, *Emergency Supplemental Appropriations Legislation for Disaster Assistance: Summary Data*, by Justin Murray and Bruce R. Lindsay. For a map of disaster declarations, see http://www.bakerprojects.com.fema/Maps/CONUS.pdf.

[5] Rutherford H. Platt, *Disasters and Democracy: The Politics of Extreme Natural Events*, (Washington, DC: Island Press, 1999), p. 66.

[6] 42 U.S.C. § 5170.

[7] 42 U.S.C. § 5191.

[8] Michael J. Trebilcock and Ronald J. Daniels, "Rationales and Instruments for Government Intervention in Natural Disasters" in Ronald J. Daniels, Donald F. Kettl, and Howard Kunreuther, eds., *On Risk and Disaster: Lessons from Hurricane Katrina*, (Philadelphia: University of Pennsylvania Press, 2006), p. 104. For additional discussion of the evolution of emergency management see Claire B. Rubin, ed. *Emergency Management: The American Experience 1900-2005* (Fairfax, VA: Public Entity Risk Institute, 2007).

[9] U.S. Department of Homeland Security, Federal Emergency Management Agency, Annual Report of FOIA Activity for FY2000, II. C., at http://www.fema.gov/doc/help/foiareportfy00.doc.

[10] U.S. Department of Homeland Security, Federal Emergency Management Agency, *Preliminary Damage Assessment Reports*, at http://www.fema.gov/rebuild/recover/pda-reports.shtm.

[11] Ibid.; and Platt, p. 266.

[12] U.S. Government Accountability Office, *Disaster Assistance: Improvements Needed in Disaster Declaration Criteria and Eligibility Assurance Procedures,* GAO-01-837, August, 2001, p. 2.

[13] For more information on emergency supplemental spending for disasters see CRS Report RL33226, *Emergency Supplemental Appropriations Legislation for Disaster Assistance: Summary Data,* by Justin Murray and Bruce R. Lindsay.

[14] U.S. Congress, House Committee on the Budget, *Budgetary Treatment of Emergencies,* p. 68, 105th Congress, 2nd. Sess., June 23, 1998 (Washington: GPO, 1998).

[15] For more information, see CRS Report RL33053, *Federal Stafford Act Disaster Assistance: Presidential Declarations, Eligible Activities, and Funding,* by Keith Bea.

[16] Ibid.; and Platt, p. 10.

[17] U.S. Congress, Senate Committee on Appropriations, Subcommittee on VA, HUD and Independent Agencies, *Departments of Veterans Affairs and Housing and Urban Development and Independent Agencies Appropriations for Fiscal Year 2002,* 107th Congress, 1st sess., p. 252, at http://www.access.gpo.gov/congress/senate.

[18] Opening Statement of Rep. Bennie Thompson, in U.S. Congress, House Committee on Homeland Security, *Disaster Declarations, Where is FEMA in a Time of Need?,* 110th Congress, 1st. sess., March 15, 2007.

[19] P.L. 110-28, 121 Stat. 155.

[20] U.S. Congress, House Committee on Appropriations, *Making Emergency Supplemental Appropriations for the Fiscal Year ending September 30, 2007 and other purposes, report to accompany H.R. 1591,* 110th Cong., 1st sess., March 20, 2007, H.Rept. 110-60, p. 211.

[21] Government Accountability Office, *FEMA Disaster Cost Estimates,* Feb. 2008, p. 4.

[22] Matt Korade, "FEMA's Success Hinges on Regional Personnel," *Congressional Quarterly,* March 16, 2010, at http://homeland.cq.com/hs/display/do?docid=3569657&sourcetype=31.

[23] P.L. 109-295, 689g, 120 Stat. 1453.

[24] For more information see CRS Report RL33729, *Federal Emergency Management Policy Changes After Hurricane Katrina: A Summary of Statutory Provisions,* coordinated by Keith Bea.

[25] U.S. Congress, House Subcommittee on Investigations and Oversight, *The Federal Emergency Management Agency's Proposed Disaster Relief Regulations,* 100th Cong., 1st sess. (Washington: GPO, 1987), pp. 3-5.

[26] 42 U.S.C. 5163.

[27] For more information, see CRS Report RL33090, *Robert T. Stafford Disaster Relief and Emergency Assistance Act: Legal Requirements for Federal and State Roles in Declarations of an Emergency or a Major Disaster,* by Elizabeth B. Bazan.

[28] 42 U.S.C. §5191.

[29] President Carter (Georgia), President Reagan (California), President Clinton (Arkansas), and President George W. Bush (Texas).

[30] Ibid.; and Platt, p. 20.

[31] CFR 44 § 206.38.

[32] CFR 44 § 206.33.

[33] Richard Sylves, Quick Response Report #86: *The Politics and Administration of Presidential Disaster Declarations: The California Floods of Winter 1995,* at http://www.colorado.edu/hazards/research/qr/qr86.html.

[34] 44 CFR §206.33(c).

[35] FEMA has 10 regional offices: Region 1 (Boston, MA), Region 2 (New York, NY), Region 3 (Philadelphia, PA), Region 4 (Atlanta, GA), Region 5 (Chicago, IL), Region 6 (Denton,

TX), Region 7 (Kansas City, MO), Region 8 (Denver, CO), Region 9 (Oakland, CA), and Region 10 (Bothell, WA).

[36] Sally Kestin and Megan O'Matz, "FEMA ruled on disaster before verifying Dade damage," *South Florida Sun-Sentinel*, at http://www.sun-sentinel.com/news/sfl-fema15may15,0, 6848867.story?coll=sfla-news-utilities.

[37] U.S. Department of Homeland Security, Federal Emergency Management Agency, "Joint State-Federal Preliminary Damage Assessment Teams Visit Flood-Damaged Communities," Release Number R10-06-047, November 13, 2006, at http://www.fema.gov /news/newsrelease.fema?id=31509.

[38] 44 CFR 206.33(d)

[39] Ibid.; and Sylves, p. 5.

[40] U.S. Department of Homeland Security, Federal Emergency Management Agency, *Presidential Declarations: What Does This Mean for Me?*, at http://www.fema.gov/ media/archives/2007/010807b.shtm.

[41] U.S. Department of Homeland Security, Federal Emergency Management Agency, "Notice of Adjustment of Statewide Per Capita Impact Indicator," 75 *Federal Register,* 62135, October 7, 2010.

[42] U.S. Census Bureau, *State & County Quick Facts,* at http://quickfacts.census.gov/gfd/states/ 06000.html.

[43] 42 U.S.C. §5170.

[44] 44 CFR § 206.48.

[45] U.S. Geological Survey, Earthquake Hazards Program, "Earthquake Density Maps for the United States", at http://earthquake.usgs.gov/regional/states/us_density.php.

[46] U.S. Department of Homeland Security, Federal Emergency Management Agency, "Notice of Adjustment of Countywide Per Capita Impact Indicator," 75 *Federal Register,* 62135, October 7, 2010.

[47] For information on public insurance coverage, see "Cost of Risk Survey" conducted by the Public Entity Risk Institute (PERI) at http://www.riskinstitute.org.

[48] 44 CFR §206.253. For additional information, see CRS Report RS22945, *Flood Insurance Requirements for Stafford Act Assistance*, by Edward C. Liu.

[49] 44 CFR §206.252.

[50] 42 U.S.C. § 5170c.

[51] For more information, see CRS Report RS22268, *Repairing and Reconstructing Disaster-Damaged Roads and Bridges: The Role of Federal-Aid Highway Assistance*, by Robert S. Kirk.

[52] For additional discussion of this law, see CRS Report RL34209, *Commercial Fishery Disaster Assistance*, by Harold F. Upton.

[53] For more information, see CRS Report RS21212, *Agricultural Disaster Assistance*, by Dennis A. Shields and Ralph M. Chite.

[54] 44 CFR §206.48(b)(1).

[55] P.L. 109-295, §689g, 120 Stat. 1453.

[56] 44 CFR §206.48(b)(2).

[57] 42 U.S.C. § 5174.

[58] Richard Sylves, Quick Response Report #86: *The Politics and Administration of Presidential Disaster Declarations: The California Floods of Winter 1995*, at http://www.colorado.edu/ hazards/research/qr/qr86.html

[59] 44 CFR §206.48 (b) (4).

[60] National Emergency Management Association (NEMA) 2006 Biennial Report: Organizations and Funding for State Emergency Management and Homeland Security, (Lexington, KY: Council of State Governments).

[61] For more information on state assistance programs, refer to the following for summary information on state statutory authorities: CRS Report RL32287, *Emergency Management and Homeland Security Statutory Authorities in the States, District of Columbia, and Insular Areas: A Summary*, by Keith Bea, L. Cheryl Runyon, and Kae M. Warnock.

[62] Ibid.; and Platt, p. 65.

[63] 42 U.S.C. §5155.

[64] Liz Pulliam Weston, "Do You Really Need Disaster Insurance?," *MSN Money,* at http://moneycentral.msn.com/content/Insurance/Insureyourhome/P59648.hsp?Printer.

[65] This statement remains accurate. However, since FEMA has begun to list PDA information on its website, it should be possible to begin to assess the efficacy of the factors employed to determine IA damage and declaration criteria.

[66] For more information, see CRS Report RL33474, *Reauthorization of the National Transportation Safety Board (NTSB)*, by Bart Elias.

[67] 44 CFR § 206.48.

[68] H.R. 3377, Title III, Sec.304.

[69] U.S. Government Accountability Office, *DISASTER ASSISTANCE: Improvement Needed in Disaster Declaration Criteria and Eligibility Assurance Procedures*, GAO-01-837, August 2001, p.11.

[70] Ibid., p. 49.

[71] Ibid.; and Platt, p. 285.

In: The Catastrophic Declaration Proposal...   ISBN: 978-1-61942-264-3
Editors: Landon West and Adrian Porter © 2012 Nova Science Publishers, Inc

Chapter 4

THE NATIONAL RESPONSE FRAMEWORK: OVERVIEW AND POSSIBLE ISSUES FOR CONGRESS[*]

Bruce R. Lindsay

SUMMARY

In response to the terrorist attacks of September 11, 2001, Congress and President Bush moved to consolidate numerous federal emergency plans into a single, unified national response plan. The end product of these efforts was the National Response Plan (NRP), which established broad lines of authority for agencies responding to emergencies and major disasters.

Perceived problems with the implementation of the NRP during Hurricane Katrina led Congress to enact the Post-Katrina Management Reform Act (P.L. 109-295) to integrate preparedness and response authorities. The legislation directed DHS to issue a successor plan to the NRP entitled the National Response Framework (NRF). Implemented in March 2008, the NRF establishes a new approach to coordinating federal and nonfederal resources and entities. The Department of Homeland Security (DHS) maintains that the NRF is an improvement over the NRP. Some, however, assert that the NRF is not an improvement because it

---

[*] This is an edited, reformatted and augmented version of a Congressional Research Service publication, CRS Report for Congress RL34758, from www.crs.gov, dated January 21, 2011.

does not fully address the problems and challenges associated with the NRP.

This report discusses how national response planning documents have evolved over time and describes the authorities that shape the NRF. Several issue areas that might be examined for potential lawmaking and oversight concerning the NRF are also highlighted.

INTRODUCTION

Congress and President Bush devoted considerable attention to how the nation can best prevent, prepare for, respond to, and recover from natural and human-caused disasters. Events such as the terrorist attacks of September 11, 2001, and Hurricane Katrina of August 2005, prompted Congress and President Bush to require the development of a plan for how government at all levels, and also the nongovernmental sector, should respond to all types of emergencies and disasters. Pursuant to statutory requirements and presidential directives, the Federal Emergency Management Agency (FEMA), an agency located within the Department of Homeland Security (DHS), issued such a plan in March 2008 with publication of the *National Response Framework* (NRF).[1]

The NRF is the end product of a long history. Prior to the terrorist attacks of September 11, 2001, the structure for responding to emergencies and disasters resided in at least 5 separate plans.[2] With the Homeland Security Act of 2002 (P.L. 107-296) and Sections 15 and 16 of the Homeland Security Presidential Directive 5 (hereafter HSPD-5), Congress and President Bush directed DHS to consolidate these plans and create a single, overarching, integrated, and coordinated national response plan, and to develop a National Incident Management System (NIMS).[3] These efforts culminated in the initial *National Response Plan* (NRP) on October 10, 2003, followed by the release of NIMS on March 1, 2004.

In August 2005, Hurricane Katrina made landfall, followed shortly by Hurricanes Rita and Wilma. A number of studies on the responses to these hurricanes found shortcomings in the NRP itself and its implementation.[4] DHS made the decision to revise the NRP partially based on these reports. The revision of the NRP was also due to mandates in the Post-Katrina Emergency Management Reform Act of 2006 (P.L. 109-295, hereafter the Post-Katrina Act). In January 2008, DHS issued the NRF, which took effect in March 2008. Since that time, the NRF has been the nation's core response document, providing a structure for the response to such disasters as the 2008 Midwest floods and California wildfires, as well as Hurricanes Gustav and Ike.

This report reviews selected statutory provisions related to the NRF and provides an overview of the document. It discusses some of the reasons the Bush Administration revised the NRP, as well as some controversial aspects of the review process. The report also summarizes selected pending legislation concerning national response planning and concludes with a discussion of issues over which Congress might consider exercising oversight.

AUTHORITIES ESTABLISHING AND INFLUENCING THE NRF

Authority for the creation of the NRF emanates from numerous sources. FEMA has described the NRF as being guided by 15 "principal emergency authorities," 48 other statutory authorities and regulations, 17 executive orders, and 20 presidential directives.[5] This report does not offer an exhaustive overview of these authorities. Rather, this section discusses some of the major authorities establishing the NRF, legislation that shaped the development of the NRF, and legislation tied to congressional oversight.

Pre-Hurricane Katrina

The Robert T. Stafford Disaster Relief and Emergency Assistance Act (hereafter the Stafford Act) establishes the programs and processes by which the federal government provides emergency and major disaster assistance to states and localities, individuals, and qualified private nonprofit organizations. Section 611 of the Stafford Act authorizes the Director of FEMA[6] to prepare federal response plans and programs and to coordinate these plans with state efforts.[7] Consistent with this authorization, FEMA released the *Federal Response Plan* in April 1992. The primary purpose of the *Federal Response Plan* was to maximize the availability of federal resources to support response and recovery efforts taken by state and local emergency officials.

After the terrorist attacks of September 11, Congress passed the Homeland Security Act of 2002 (P.L. 107-296). Subsection 502(6) required the consolidation of "existing federal government emergency response plans into a single, coordinated national response plan."[8] The Homeland Security Act also created DHS, consolidating over 20 agencies, including FEMA, into a single department. Under DHS, FEMA retained both its authority to administer the provisions of the Stafford Act and its designation as the lead agency for the nation's response plan.

On February 28, 2003, President Bush issued HSPD-5. Section 16 of HSPD-5 directed the Secretary to develop and submit for review to the Homeland Security Council a national response plan. Section 16 also mandated that the plan use an "all-discipline" and "all-hazards" approach in preparing for, responding to, and recovering from domestic incidents.[9] In December 2004, through the primary guidance and authorization of the Stafford Act, the Homeland Security Act, and HSPD-5, DHS issued a successor to the *Federal Response Plan*, which was entitled the *National Response Plan* (NRP).[10]

Post-Hurricane Katrina

The NRP was in place and implemented for the Hurricane Katrina response in August 2005. The problems that arose from Hurricane Katrina prompted numerous studies. Some of these studies attributed the poor response, in part, to the implementation of the NRP. Concerned by perceived deficiencies in the NRP, Congress sought a remedy through legislation in the Post-Katrina Act. The Post-Katrina Act provides the most comprehensive legislation concerning the NRP (or any subsequent plans) by mandating numerous adjustments to the NRP as well as mechanisms for oversight. Section 642 amended the Stafford Act and the Homeland Security Act to mandate that the President develop a national preparedness system.[11] Section 643 further establishes that the President shall, through the Administrator of FEMA "complete, revise, and update, as necessary, a national preparedness goal... to ensure the Nation's ability to prevent, respond to, recover from, and mitigate against natural disasters, acts of terrorism, and other man-made disasters."[12] It further states that the national preparedness goal, to the extent possible, should be consistent with NIMS and the NRP.

Section 649(b) of the Post-Katrina Act requires that the national preparedness goal, NIMS, and the NRP be subjected to clear and quantifiable performance measures to ensure they are continuously revised and updated.[13] Section 652 of the act establishes annual reporting requirements concerning preparedness capabilities.[14] Section 652(c) requires the reporting of state compliance with the NRP.[15] Finally, Section 653 requires the president to ensure that federal agencies assigned with responsibilities in the NRP have the capability to meet the national preparedness goal, and develop plans to "respond effectively to natural disasters, acts of terrorism, and other man-made disasters in support of the National Response Plan to ensure a coordinated federal response."[16]

In response to the Post-Katrina legislation and perceived problems with the implementation of the NRP, DHS revised the plan and issued the NRF. The following section describes the various components of the document.

OVERVIEW OF THE NRF

General Approach

The NRF is part of a national strategy for homeland security. It provides the doctrine and guiding principles for a unified response from all levels of government, and all sectors of communities, to all types of hazards regardless of their origin.[17] Although the primary focus of the NRF is on response and short-term recovery, the document also defines the roles and responsibilities of the various actors involved in all phases of emergency management.[18]

The NRF is not an operational plan that dictates a step-by-step process for responding to hazards. Rather, the NRF appears to be an attempt to build flexibility into response efforts by setting up a framework that DHS believes is necessary for responding to hazards. Within this framework, the NRF gives users a degree of discretion as to how they choose to respond to the incident.

Components of the NRF Document

The NRF is organized into five parts. The introductory chapter presents an overview of the entire document and explains the evolution of the NRF, and identifies the various actors involved in emergency and disaster response. The chapter also discusses the concepts undergirding emergency preparedness and response by providing a list of what DHS describes as the "five key principles" of response doctrine.[19]

The first chapter of the NRF, entitled "Roles and Responsibilities," provides an overview of the roles and responsibilities of federal, state, and local governments, the nonprofit and private sectors, and individuals and households. The first chapter also discusses the roles and responsibilities of those who hold various positions within these entities.

The second chapter, entitled "Response Actions," describes and outlines key tasks as they pertain to what DHS calls the "three phases of effective response." These phases include "prepare," "respond," and "recover." Preparing includes planning, organizing, equipping, training, exercising, and conducting evaluations. Activities related to responding include gaining and maintaining situational awareness,[20] activating and deploying resources and capabilities, coordinating response actions, and demobilizing. "Recover" activities are broken down into two broad categories. These are short-term and long-term recovery.

The third chapter of the NRF, entitled "Response Organization," discusses the organizational structure and staffing used to implement response actions, all of which are based on NIMS and ICS.[21] The NRF describes the organization and staffing structure of every entity responsible for preparedness and response in detail.

The fourth chapter, entitled "Planning," describes the process of planning as it pertains to national preparedness and summarizes planning structures relative to the NRF. The chapter describes the criteria for successful planning and offers example scenarios for planning.

The fifth and final chapter of the NRF, entitled "Additional Resources," describes the 15 Emergency Support Function (ESF) Annexes to the NRF, eight Support Annexes, and seven Incident Annexes.[22] These annexes are listed in *Table A-1* and *Table A-2* of this report. The final chapter also explains that the NRF and its annexes are posted online through the *NRF Resource Center,* which allows for ongoing revisions to the document.[23]

Reasons for Replacing the NRP

As mentioned earlier in the report, several studies attributed the problematic response to Hurricane Katrina partly to the implementation of the NRP. Although the NRP was used for smaller emergencies and disasters prior to Hurricane Katrina, the hurricane marked the first time the NRP was used for a catastrophic incident. The section that follows discusses how some of the changes in the NRF have addressed these criticisms.

Difficulty in Understanding the NRP

The NRP was widely criticized as complicated and overly bureaucratic. Some said it was long and weighed down with technical language. Additionally, users of the NRP reported that the document failed to clarify roles and responsibilities and that the federal chain of command was confusing.[24] It was further pointed out that the name "National Response Plan" was a misnomer (and hence misleading) because it was not a true operational plan in the sense that it did not provide a step-by-step process for responding to an incident.

The NRF uses less technical language than the NRP, and attempts to make the roles and responsibilities more transparent. The NRF is also shorter. Whereas the NRP contained over 400 pages, the NRF is roughly 80 pages. Still, some have contested the clarity of the NRF. This will be discussed in greater detail later in the report.

National Versus Federal Focus

Despite efforts to make the NRP a nationwide response plan, the NRP was widely seen as not sufficiently national in its focus because it emphasized federal preparedness and response. Some have further argued that the process of creating the plan excluded nonfederal stakeholders, such as states and localities.[25]

According to DHS, the NRF more clearly articulates the roles and responsibilities of nonfederal entities.[26] Additionally, when drafting the NRF, DHS held outreach sessions to solicit the feedback of nonfederal partners.[27] The extent of nonfederal participation in the creation of the NRF has been questioned and is discussed later in this report.

Progress on the NRF Since Hurricane Katrina

Several emergencies and disasters have taken place since implementation of the NRF. In general, responses to the NRF have been mixed. Some have indicated that its implementation has been successful.[28] One observer stated that coordination among federal, state, and local governments has improved.[29] In the case of Hurricanes Gustav and Ike, officials in Texas related that the federal response to the hurricanes was good.[30] Other officials have been ambivalent regarding implementation of the NRF, noting that the scale of recent disasters has not warranted enough federal involvement to understand how well the NRF works.[31]

A review of various reports may hint at some problems, however. For instance, during Hurricanes Gustav and Ike, state officials in Texas said it was the local government's responsibility to set up distribution points for supplies. However, the local government claimed it was unaware of this responsibility.[32] Such confusion may indicate that the NRF still does not clearly articulate the roles and responsibilities of state and local governments during emergencies and disasters.

Other, more serious criticisms of the NRF have surfaced since its implementation. A report issued by the Inspector General of DHS stated that some of the decisions made by FEMA during the response to Hurricane Ike did not adhere to certain principles set forth in the NRF.[33] The following section discusses these in greater depth and highlights issues Congress might examine or policy options it might consider.

POTENTIAL ISSUES FOR CONGRESS

Confusion Concerning the FCO and the PFO

One frequent criticism of the NRF is the ambiguity surrounding the relationship and role of the Federal Coordinating Officer (FCO) and the Principle Federal Officer (PFO).[34]

The FCO determines the types of relief most urgently needed, establishes field offices, and coordinates relief efforts.[35] The FCO position is authorized by the Stafford Act. Immediately upon declaring a major disaster, Section 302(a) of the Stafford Act requires the President to appoint an FCO.[36]

The PFO, on the other hand, is not a legislatively authorized position. Rather, the PFO position was created by DHS in the NRP. The PFO is designated by the Secretary of DHS, represents the Secretary as the leading federal official, and serves as the primary point of contact for state and local officials. During Hurricane Katrina, Michael Brown, who was serving as the Director of FEMA, was additionally designated as the PFO. William Lokey served as the FCO for Louisiana. To some observers (such as the Inspector general for DHS), these roles created a great deal of confusion during Hurricane Katrina, because it appeared that two people were in charge of the relief operations.[37]

Despite criticisms of the position, DHS made the decision to retain the PFO in the NRF. The decision spurred congressional concern prompting several attempts to clarify or abolish the PFO position.[38] For example, Section

526 of the Consolidated Appropriations Act, 2008 (P.L. 110-161) states that "none of the funds provided by this or previous appropriations Acts shall be used to fund any position designated as a Principal Federal Official for any Robert T. Stafford Disaster Relief and Emergency Assistance Act declared disasters or emergencies."

Persistent congressional oversight and legislative efforts may have resolved the issue. In a hearing before the Subcommittee on Economic Development, Public Buildings, and Emergency Management Committee on Transportation and Infrastructure FEMA Administrator Craig Fugate stated that DHS has determined that the PFO position would not be used for an emergency or major disaster under the Stafford Act and that planning and response documents were in the process of being updated to reflect that decision.[39]

Integrating Nonfederal Stakeholders in National Planning

A criticism of the NRP was that input from nonfederal stakeholders, such as state and local governments, nonprofit groups, and the private sector, was poorly integrated into the document. Congress addressed this issue in Section 653 of the Post-Katrina Act, where Congress required DHS and FEMA to develop operational plans with state, local, and tribal government officials.[40] According to a GAO report, DHS initially included nonfederal stakeholder input in the creation of the NRF, but later "deviated" from the process.[41] Rather than disseminating the first draft of the NRF to stakeholders, DHS conducted an internal review of the document. GAO found that the issuance of a later draft to nonfederal stakeholders was delayed, reducing the amount of time for the stakeholders to respond with comments on the draft. Additionally, GAO reported that DHS failed to establish FEMA's National Advisory Council (NAC) by the December 2006 deadline that was set forth in Section 508 of the Post-Katrina Act. According to the act, the NAC is responsible for incorporating the input of state, local, and tribal governments and the private sector in the development and revision of the NRF.[42]

The importance of meeting the congressional mandate has been addressed by one analyst. Donald Kettl, a public policy professor at the University of Pennsylvania, has emphasized the importance of including local officials in the planning process. According to Kettl, "no amount of national planning can side-step the fact that ... the first indicator that something bad is happening is a report from the frontlines."[43]

In consideration of these conclusions, some may argue that failing to integrate feedback from local emergency officials could (1) omit hazards that are known at the local level but not recognized by federal officials, (2) miss an opportunity to integrate the lessons learned from local responders who have first-hand experience with emergencies and disasters, and (3) fail to establish "buy-in" to the plan at the state and local level thereby creating a possible reluctance to execute the plan faithfully. If the issue of nonfederal stakeholder input were of concern to Congress, it might move to conduct oversight on the extent to which DHS and FEMA are utilizing the NAC and incorporating nonfederal stakeholders in all aspects of national emergency planning and revision.

Children and Disasters

In testimony before the House Homeland Security Subcommittee on Emergency Preparedness, Science and Technology, one emergency professional[44] pointed out that there is a gap in the level of emergency readiness between adult and pediatric care.[45] He noted that children are more vulnerable to hazardous materials than adults, have unique treatment needs, and require care from providers who have been specifically trained to meet these needs. The witness stated, however, that federal, state, and local efforts in disaster planning have generally overlooked the unique needs of children.

Separately, Mark Shriver, Vice President and Managing Director of Save the Children's U.S. Programs, has stated that children are vulnerable during emergencies and evacuations. According to Shriver, the needs of children are commonly overlooked before, during, and after a disaster. Shelters, for example, often have unsanitary conditions, and many communities lack sufficient stockpiles of diapers, formula, pediatric medications, and child-size respirators.[46]

In various legislative provisions, Congress has focused on the needs of children during disasters. For example, the Post-Katrina Act contains a provision to reunite children with their families by establishing, within the National Center for Missing and Exploited Children, a new National Emergency Child Locator Center.[47] Congress addressed the subject again in the Consolidated Appropriations Act, 2008. Division G, Section 603 of the act establishes the National Commission on Children and Disasters. The purpose of the Commission is to conduct a comprehensive study to examine and assess the needs of children during disasters and submit a report to the President and Congress.[48]

Under the NRF, the needs of children are addressed in ESF #6 and #13.[49] The support of children's needs in ESF #6 is delegated to several nonprofit organizations, including Catholic Charities, Feed the Children, Save the Children, and the United Methodist Committee on Relief (UMCOR). One of the functions of ESF #13 is to protect children. Under the annex, the National Center for Missing and Exploited Children (NCMEC), a private sector organization, is responsible for preventing child abduction and sexual exploitation, and helping locate missing children.

Congress might consider how well the issue of child protection in disasters is addressed in the NRF annexes. Several observations about the NRF's current coverage include the following.

First, there are no primary agencies designated as responsible for addressing children's needs. Only supporting agencies have this designation. Second, some may argue that the annexes are flawed because the Public Health and Medical Services Annex (ESF #8) and Search and Rescue Annex (ESF #9) do not explicitly mention children in their various functions. Third, some may argue that having multiple annexes focused on the needs of children may create service gaps, and that when several organizations are assigned with responsibility, it becomes unclear what agency will take the lead, and what functions these agencies are carrying out. In addition, they may argue that having multiple organizations creates unnecessary duplication.

The NRF as a Living Document

Having the NRF available online appears to have some benefits. Emergencies and disasters are fluid events and having a document capable of adapting to the needs created by unique emergencies and disasters would seem to add a degree of flexibility to the NRF. It also gives users easy access to the document. Users can also sign up for email alerts to be informed of changes in the NRF. However, it is unclear what mechanisms are in place to ensure users who visit the website infrequently, or do not sign up for alerts, are informed of NRF modifications or changes. Is it possible that a state or locality may use protocols that have been removed or revised?

The NRF is always in effect, whereas the NRP had to be invoked when an emergency or disaster struck. According to DHS, this has the benefit of speeding response time because it eliminates the need to wait for some form of announcement that the plan is in effect. Some may argue that a plan that is always in effect lacks a triggering mechanism to alert responders and create situational awareness. Does the NRF benefit response activities by always being in effect?

Reporting Requirements and Metrics

The Post-Katrina Act requires the Administrator of FEMA to submit to Congress annual reports that identify the resources needed to enhance regional offices and undertake planning, training, surge capacity, and logistics. Reporting must also include information about state compliance with the NRF and the extent to which the use of federal assistance during the preceding fiscal year achieved preparedness priorities.[50] Additionally, homeland security grants require broad state compliance with national preparedness policy.

Some may argue that emergency management practices are strengthened when states and localities adopt federal standards for emergency preparedness and response. Others may argue that mandating compliance has at least two negative consequences. First, not all states have the same set of hazards. A one-size-fits-all approach may not be the best method of addressing hazards, because states and localities are better positioned to make decisions about how to conduct emergency planning and response.[51] Second, requiring compliance and creating standards increases federal involvement in emergency policy. Again, some may argue this is beneficial, because it can help save lives and reduce property loss, but others might argue that the requirements infringe on state sovereignty.

Emphasis on Terrorism

Incident Annexes in the NRF are primarily oriented toward terrorism. Since Hurricane Katrina, some have argued that there has been an emphasis on planning for high-impact, low-probability incidents at the expense of low-impact, high-probability incidents. Additionally, it is possible that planning for terrorism underemphasizes preparedness for natural disasters. For example, in testimony before the House Natural Resources Committee, David Applegate pointed out that earthquakes are among the most expensive of natural disasters in terms of destruction. According to Applegate, this underscores the importance of preparedness and mitigation; however, there is no Incident Annex addressing earthquakes.[52] Concern over a potential earthquake on the New Madrid fault line has persuaded officials to use an earthquake scenario for the 2011 National Level Exercise in Arkansas. An earthquake annex could be used to guide the exercise and assess response capabilities.

The President of the International Association of Emergency Managers (IAEM) and Director of Emergency Management, Hillsborough County, Florida, also addressed the terrorism emphasis. Director Larry Gispert responded favorably to President-elect Obama's plan to support first-responders, prepare effective emergency response plans, improve interoperable communications systems, and work with state and local governments and the private sector, and allocate funds based on risk. Gispert objected to plans that focus on terrorism because state and local emergency managers primarily deal with natural disasters. According to Gispert, the plan would have the benefit of allowing state and local governments to prepare for both types of incidents rather than predominantly terrorism.[53]

On the other hand, others would argue that planning for terrorism is of the utmost importance and that a terrorist attack would have the same consequences as a natural disaster.[54] They may conclude that planning and preparedness for terrorism can be applied toward natural disasters and therefore fits the all-hazards model of emergency management.

If Congress were concerned about the possibility that preparedness for natural disasters is being hampered by overemphasizing terrorism in emergency plans, or that resources for natural disaster preparedness are being diverted to prepare for terrorist events, Congress may elect to have FEMA develop natural disaster annexes, or incorporate more natural disaster planning in existing Incident Annexes.

CONCLUDING OBSERVATIONS

In response to directives from Congress and the President, the Bush Administration issued the NRF to establish a new approach to coordinate federal and nonfederal entities in times of emergencies and major disasters. The NRF does appear to respond to some of the challenges identified by Congress and others. The document is more concise, has less jargon, and has made an attempt to clarify roles and responsibilities. Additionally, anecdotal reports following Gustav and Ike indicate the coordination of emergency activities among federal, state, and local governments has improved.

On the other hand, parts of the NRF may have retained some of the problems associated with the NRP. The NRF still contains the PFO arrangement, terrorism and natural disasters are not given equal treatment, and nonfederal stakeholder input appears to be lacking.

APPENDIX. ANNEXES TO THE NATIONAL RESPONSE FRAMEWORK

Table A-1. List of ESF Annexes

Emergency Support Function (ESF) Annexes	
ESF #1	Transportation
ESF #2	Communications
ESF #3	Public Works and Engineering
ESF #4	Firefighting
ESF #5	Emergency Management
ESF #6	Mass Care, Emergency Assistance, Housing, and Human Services
ESF #7	Logistics Management and Resource Support
ESF #8	Public Health and Medical Services
ESF #9	Search and Rescue
ESF #10	Oil and Hazardous Materials Response
ESF #11	Agriculture and Natural Resources
ESF #12	Energy
ESF #13	Public Safety and Security
ESF #14	Long-Term Community Recovery
ESF #15	External Affairs

Table A-2. Lists of Incident and Support Annexes

Incident Annexes
Biological Incident
Catastrophic Incident
Cyber Incident
Food and Agriculture Incident
Mass Evacuation Incident
Nuclear/Radiological Incident
Terrorism Incident Law Enforcement and Investigation
Support Annexes
Critical Infrastructure and Key Resources
Financial Management
International Coordination
Private-Sector Coordination
Public Affairs
Tribal Relations
Volunteer and Donations Management
Worker Safety and Health

Some may contend that insufficient implementation studies have been conducted on the NRF to assess its efficacy. Others might argue the NRF has yet to be tested by a large-scale disaster to form a clear picture of its effectiveness; the only way to find out whether the NRF is an improvement over the NRP may be to subject it to a major catastrophe comparable to Hurricanes Andrew or Katrina

End Notes

[1] U.S. Department of Homeland Security, Federal Emergency Management Agency, National Response Framework (Washington: January 2008), http://www.fema.gov/pdf/emergency/nrf/nrf-core.pdf.

[2] These were the Federal Response Plan (which provided an overall plan for federal response since 1992), Conplan, Radiological Plan, National Contingency Plan, and Distant Shores. Certain aspects of these plans were integrated or linked to the national plan through the use of annexes.

[3] NIMS is a preparedness and response model that uses standardized terminology, communication systems, and organizational structures for a unified response. NIMS was created to integrate effective practices in emergency preparedness and response into a national framework for incident management.

[4] These include U.S. Congress, Senate Committee on Homeland Security and Governmental Affairs, Hurricane Katrina: A Nation Still Unprepared, 109th Cong., 2nd sess., S.Rept. 109-322 (Washington: GPO, 2006); U.S. Congress, House Select Bipartisan Committee to Investigate the Preparation for and Response to Hurricane Katrina, A Failure of Initiative: Final Report of the House Select Bipartisan Committee to Investigate the Preparation for and Response to Hurricane Katrina, 109th Cong., 2nd sess., H.Rept. 109-377 (Washington: GPO, 2006), and the White House Homeland Security Council, The Federal Response to Hurricane Katrina: Lessons Learned (Washington: February 23, 2006).

[5] U.S. Department of Homeland Security, Federal Emergency Management Agency, National Response Framework: List of Authorities and References, January 2008, pp. 1-16, http://www.fema.gov/pdf/emergency/nrf/nrf-authorities.pdf.

[6] Section 612(c) of the Post-Katrina Act renamed the position of Director to Administrator.

[7] 42 U.S.C. 5196(b).

[8] 6 U.S.C. 312.

[9] U.S. President (G.W. Bush) Homeland Security Presidential Directive 5, sect. 16.

[10] U.S. Department of Homeland Security, National Response Plan (Washington: December 2004), http://www.scd.state.hi.us/documents/nrp.pdf.

[11] 6 U.S.C. 742, 120 Stat. 1425.

[12] 6 U.S.C. 743, 120 Stat. 1425.

[13] 6 U.S.C. 749, 120 Stat. 1428.

[14] 6 U.S.C. 749, 120 Stat. 1429.

[15] 6 U.S.C. 752, 120 Stat. 1430.

[16] 6 U.S.C. 753. Sec. 653(a)(4), 120 Stat. 1431.

[17] U.S. Department of Homeland Security, "National Response Framework Released," press release, January 22, 2008, http://www.dhs.gov/xnews/releases/pr_1201030569827.shtm.

[18] These phases are mitigation, prevention, response, and recovery.

[19] These are:

    (1)   Engaged Partnership: the NRF advocates for open lines of communication among various emergency management entities and for support partnerships during preparedness activities so that when incidents take place, these various entities are able to work together.

    (2)   Tiered Response: responses to incidents begin at the local level. When local capacity is overwhelmed, state authorities assist the locality. Likewise, should the state be overwhelmed, assistance from the federal government is requested.

    (3)   Scalable, Flexible, and Adaptable Operational Capabilities: as incidents change in size, scope, and complexity, there needs to be a corresponding change in the response apparatus.

    (4)   Unity of Effort Through Unified Command: a clear understanding of the roles and responsibilities of each entity is necessary for effective response. Moreover, effective response requires a unit of effort within the emergency management chain of command.

    (5)   Readiness to Act: all emergency management agencies, to the extent possible should anticipate incidents and make preparations to respond swiftly to them.

[20] "Situational awareness" refers to monitoring information regarding actual and developing incidents.

[21] ICS establishes a management system that helps agencies responding to an incident work together in a coordinated and systematic approach.

[22] ESFs provide the structure for coordinating federal interagency support for responses involving multiple federal agencies. Support Annexes describe how federal, state, tribal, and local entities, as well as nongovernmental organizations (NGOs) and the private sector, coordinate and execute the common functional processes and administrative requirements for incident management. Incident Annexes are specific hazard scenarios that require specialized and specific response efforts.

[23] NRF Resource Center, http://www.fema.gov/emergency/nrf/#.

[24] Thomas Birkland and Sarah Waterman "Is Federalism the Reason for Policy Failure in Hurricane Katrina?," Publius, vol. 38, no. 4 (Fall, 2008), p. 706.

[25] Based on a discussion with James Kish, Senior Director, Exercises and Evaluations, DHS February 2008.

[26] U.S. Department of Homeland Security, National Response Framework (Washington: January 2008), p. 2.

[27] Mickey McCarter, "FEMA Deputy Director Lauds National Response Framework," Homeland Security Today, September 30, 2007, http://www.hstoday.us/ content/ view/205/128/.

[28] For example see, Daniel Fowler, "Effective Response to Gustav—Courting Complacency or Heralding a Habit?" CQ Press, September 3, 2008, http://homeland.cq.com/hs/displayalert. do?matchId=64477887.

[29] Daniel Fowler, "Who's in Charge Still a Disaster-Response Question Mark," CQ Homeland Security, September 22, 2008.

[30] Daniel Fowler, "Federal Response to Recent Hurricanes Termed 'So Far, So Good'," CQ Homeland Security, September 23, 2008.

[31] Based on telephone conversations with emergency managers in Maine, New Mexico, Oregon, and North Dakota.

[32] Daniel Fowler, "Who's in Charge Still a Disaster-Response Question Mark," CQ Press, September 22, 2008.

[33] Richard L. Skinner, Management Advisory Report: FEMA's Response to Hurricane Ike, Department of Homeland Security: Office of Inspector General, Washington, DC, June 11, 2009, http://www.dhs.gov/xoig/assets/mgmtrpts/OIG_09_78_June09.pdf.

[34] For example see U.S. Congress, Senate, Hurricane Katrina: A Nation Still Unprepared, special report of the Committee on Homeland Security and Governmental Affairs, 109th Cong., 2nd sess. (Washington: 2006), pp. 552-553.

[35] Ibid, pp. 552-553.

[36] 42 U.S.C. 5143.

[37] U.S. Department of Homeland Security, Office of Inspector General, FEMA's Preparedness for the Next Catastrophic Disaster, OIG/OIG-08-34, March 2008, p. 15, http://www.dhs.gov/xoig/assets/mgmtrpts/OIG_08-34_Mar08.pdf.

[38] Recent examples include two measures introduced in the 111th Congress: S. 412 which would have established the PFO as a subordinate authority to federal or state officials, and H.R. 1174 which would have abolished the PFO position.

[39] U.S. Congress, House Committee on Transportation and Infrastructure, Subcommittee on Economic Development, Public Buildings and Emergency Management, Priorities for Disasters and Economic Disruption: The Proposed FY2011 Budgets for FEMA and EDA, 111th Cong., 2nd sess., May 6, 2010 (Washington: GPO, 2010), p. 8.

[40] 42 U.S.C. 753.

[41] U.S. Government Accountability Office, National Response Framework: FEMA needs Policies and Procedures to Better Integrate Non-Federal Stakeholders in the Revision Process, GAO-08-768, June 2008, p. 9.

[42] Richard Skinner, the Inspector General for DHS, made the same assertion, stating that FEMA's NAC was not established in time to have meaningful input into the development of the NRF. See Testimony of the Inspector General for the Department of Homeland Security, in U.S. Congress, Senate Committee on Homeland Security and Governmental Affairs, The New FEMA: Is the Agency Better Prepared for a Catastrophe Now Than It Was in 2005?, 110th Cong., 2nd sess., April 03, 2008, http://hsgac.senate.gov/ public/_files/ 040308 Skinner.pdf.

[43] Donald F. Kettl, "Katrina Plus Three," Governing.com, August 2008. http://www.governing.com/articles/0808potomac.htm.

[44] Steven Krug is the Head of the Division of Pediatric Emergency Medicine at Children's Memorial Hospital in Chicago, Illinois, and a Professor of Pediatrics at the Northwestern University Feinberg School of Medicine.

[45] Testimony of Steven Krug, U.S. House Committee on Homeland Security, Subcommittee on Emergency Preparedness, Science and Technology, Emergency Care Crisis: A Nation Unprepared for Public Health Disasters, July 26, 2006, http://www.aap.org/sections/pem/er_readiness_testimonyfinal.pdf.

[46] Save the Children, Keeping Texas Children Safe from Hurricane Ike, September 11, 2008, http://www.savethechildren.org/newsroom/2008/texas-hurricane-ike.html.   See   also Editorial, "What About the Children? A National Commission Starts Work to Make Sure the Young Aren't Forgotten During Disasters," Washington Post, October 14, 2008, A16. http://www.washingtonpost.com/wp-dyn/content/article/2008/10/13/AR2008101302279.html.

[47] Sec. 689(b)(1).

[48] P.L. 110-161, Sec. 604(1)(2)(3).

[49] ESF #6 is the Mass Care, Emergency Assistance, Housing, and Human Services Annex and ESF #13 is the Public Safety and Security Annex.

[50] P.L. 109-295, Sec. 652(a)(2)(A)-(D), 120 Stat. 1429, Sec. 652(c)(2)(A)-(C), 120 Stat. 1430.

[51] Samuel Clovis, "Promises Unfulfilled: the Sub-Optimization of Homeland Security National Preparedness," Homeland Security Affairs, vol. 4, no. 3, October 2008. http://www.hsaj.org/pages/volume4/issue3/pdfs/4.3.3.pdf.

[52] Testimony of Director of Government Affairs, U.S. Geological Survey U.S. Department of the Interior, David Applegate, in U.S. Congress, House Committee on Natural Resources Subcommittee on Energy and Mineral Resources, The United States Geological Survey's Earthquake Hazards Program - Science, Preparation, and Response, 110th Cong., 2nd sess., May 22, 2008, http://resourcescommittee.house.gov/images/Documents/20080522/ testimony_applegate.pdf.

[53] Daniel Fowler, "Experts Like Obama's Preparedness Plans, Eager to See the Details," CQ Press, November 11, 2008.

[54] RAND National Defense Research Institute, When It Comes to Terrorism, How Prepared Are Local and State Agencies? RB-9209-OSD (2006), http://www.rand.org/pubs/research_briefs/2006/RAND_RB9209.pdf.

INDEX